Laws For Awakening Humanity

HIGHER LAWS OF SPIRIT

~

LAWS OF SOUL LIFE

~

EIGHT QUALITIES OF GROUP ACTIVITY

~

A BANNER FOR THE NEW ERA

THREE DISCIPLES

email: contact@lawsforawakeninghumanity.org
website: lawsforawakeninghumanity.org

DEDICATION

To the Creator of All.

~

To The Holy Ones,
Boddhisattvas,
Masters and Saints.

~

To Enlightenment
Arising Within the Lotus
of Human Consciousness.

~

The Peace of Spirit
is Within

CONTENTS

II - Higher Laws of Spirit:
1. Law of Love, 2. Law of Cause and Effect, 3. Law of Rebirth, 4. Law of Antithesis, 5. Law of Alignment, 6. Law of Perfection, 7. Law of Goal-Fitness and Co-Measurement, 8. Law of Detachment, 9. Law of Resonance, 10. Law of Substance, 11. Law of Death, 12. Law of Supply and Demand, 13. Law of Gravitation, 14. Law of Magnetic Control, 15. Law of Enlightenment, 16. Law of Hierarchy, 17. Law of Polarity, 18. Laws of Electricity, 19. Law of Cycles, 20. Laws of Universal Harmonics, 21. Law of Universality, 22. Law of Group Dharma, 23. Laws of Manifestation, 24. Law of The Christos, 25. Law of Evolution, 26. Law of Recognition, 27. Law of Analogy 28. Law of Unity, 29. Law of Vibration, 30. Law of Cohesion, 31. Law of Rhythm, 32. Law of Loving Understanding, 33. Law of Assembly.

III - Laws of Soul Life: 34. Law of Sacrifice, 35. Law of Magnetic Impulse, 36. Law of Service, 37. Law of Repulse, 38. Law of Elevation, 39. Law of Expansive Response, 40. Law of the Lower Four.

ACKNOWLEDGMENTS

This book has been a wonderful experience in understanding and communicating a profound, yet esoteric subject. The gems of the Ageless Wisdom need to be made more accessible, especially in this time of spiritual awakening, when human collaboration with Elders[1] of the Fifth Kingdom is growing and their presence is being felt. They are selfless, illumined souls that draw from a living source of love and truth, who guide humanity with wisdom and compassion.

As long as there is growth in a spiritual direction, the ancient adage is true: knowledge, when applied becomes wisdom, and where there is wisdom, there is also love. The authors are grateful for having learned the value of "when applied" from their experience with the wisdom of Elders.

Three individuals have authored this first edition of Laws For Awakening Humanity. One of the three, a conscious channel, received information foundational to the project. One researched and coordinated material on the subject. One provided editing, proof-reading and contributed original content. One was skilled in typing, book and website design. All three contributed in ways best suited to the needs of the project. But, who did what and what their names are, really is of no consequence. The book is considered a product of group unity. Thus, the co-authors, each wish to be known, simply as a disciple[2] of the spiritual path.

Members of the Fifth Kingdom may say they are not all-knowing or perfect, but they are wise and loving beyond human comprehension. For their love and guidance, always plumb, level and true, the authors are eternally grateful, and to all the fearless souls on the planet who keep the fires of love burning: "Thank you. TOGETHER, in a joyful spirit, we are building the new world of light!"

Three Disciples

---

[1] Human beings farther along the evolutionary path of consciousness, members of the spiritual Hierarchy, the Fifth Kingdom. There are four kingdoms, physical in nature: 1. mineral, 2. vegetable, 3. animal, 4. human. The fifth kingdom is spiritual in nature.

[2] A disciple, in this case, is someone committed to walking the path of spiritual transformation, while striving to solve problems with reason, clear thinking, love and understanding.

The three co-authors are students of the Ageless Wisdom,[3] living in the end times of an age, when the eons of human selfhood is ending and a new evolutionary age is beginning: that of the soul. We can already see signs of this transition in the declarations of freedom, justice, and truth being expressed in the world as a result of this process.

Some examples are the grassroots movements around the world, working to end war and aggression, support peace and human rights initiatives and the youth, urging world leaders to take climate action. Though still unconscious, the sense of human unity is growing and this is where the divine laws come in.

This book provides the reader with an understanding of the divine laws in clear and simple language. It strives to make them understandable to those with little esoteric background. This book is also written for those who have acquired a degree of knowledge of the world's spiritual and philosophical traditions. (Though there is no glossary, there is an excellent one at https://www.atreeoflight.org/Glossary, which one of the authors helped develop. Understanding in plain language, the meaning of esoteric terms, such as "divine plan", will enable more engagement with the material in this book.)

We are living in a time of transition where we can see personality expression already being replaced by soul expression. A gentle oscillation is taking place as humanity's consciousness shifts from the third dimensional awareness of the personality to that of the soul, the true self, an expression of an even greater divine self. Preparing for this shift is one of the purposes of this book.

Laws For Awakening Humanity, first appeared on: lawsforawakeninghumanity.org, in the year 2023, but its petals had not yet fully unfolded. The 2024 publication is completely revised with new material and will continue to be offered for free on the website. It is also available in paperback and e-book formats at www.amazon.com.

The laws in this presentation do not deal with the enforcement or attitudes of man-made laws. The force of law with its penalties was a necessary stage for humanity as it evolved. The higher laws of spirit and soul life are not to be regarded as mechanical. They are divine emanations, superlatively great wills of perfect wisdom and light, functioning as universal, eternal and immutable subjective laws.

Through the efforts of many spiritual workers, there are "Three Recognitions"[4] emerging into the consciousness of humanity. They are: 1) the soul-the true self of a human being which is part of the world soul, 2) the Fifth Kingdom-the realm of spiritually evolved souls and 3) the divine plan with its nurturing divine laws. Continuing to educate the public in them is very necessary.

All of humanity is being affected by this

---

[3] a non-religious body of teachings on spirituality, the nature of reality and consciousness.

[4] The "Three Recognitions" are not the focus of this book but are related to the divine laws. They were introduced in the books by Alice A. Bailey because of the need to educate the public in them. At the end of the book, there are suggestions for further reading on this subject.

evolutionary transition with its wars, injustice and natural catastrophes. So, is there cause for real hope or despair?

If one takes the time to really consider how much truth there is in the divine laws, the Three Recognitions, and the transition the life of the planet is in, then despair has a chance of being transformed into hope, faith and trust.

The willingness to see fear, selfishness, greed, anger and irrationality for what it is and trust in an upward arc of evolution with which humanity can cooperate, cannot be forced. It must come through a change of heart and the divine human right to choose.

The natural tendency of the soul is to love, to grow and to express itself. Its nature is light and love, and it is attracted to the beauty and order of life. Alignment with divine law allows for an intimate experience of the intricate web of cosmic life, while alignment with the soul, places one in harmony with the divine.

The ageless wisdom says living energy created the divine universe as a means of expanding into matter to see how its laws would work through all levels of being. It also says that living energy expresses itself through consciousness and consciousness expresses itself through matter. Thus, form follows consciousness and consciousness constantly evolves into more perfect expressions of being. The meaning of these statements is worth pondering.

The divine laws are not meant to be followed unquestioningly or accepted at face value, but they can be used as a certain standard and measure. By studying the divine laws and how they work, we can hone our inner wisdom and utilize it for the benefit of humanity.

The divine laws are there to guide the evolution of our planet towards perfection. If there is one piece of advice that this book can offer, it is this: to be kind, compassionate, loving, giving and responsible human beings, and to continue the spiritual transformation of the ego as much as possible.

It can be a challenge to take what is esoteric and make it exoteric without diluting the wisdom. But as the ageless wisdom says, there is nothing difficult in the word of truth and that those who do not believe, cannot be persuaded. This book is for all who can hear, to facilitate the growth of consciousness in preparation for the new world of light.

(Note: the term *spiritual* as it is used throughout this presentation means: of a higher more refined nature than the material, yet related to the world of form.)

SLOKA

That which is created by the one,
the universal Law of Cosmos is not sundered
by the ordinance of cosmic energy.

Unity is manifest through all Space, and this law is reflected in
all manifestations of life.

Man alone, separating himself from the infinite energy of the
manifestation of Cosmos, is precisely eluding Truth.

Cosmos creates for Infinity. Cosmos builds with co-measurement.
Communion is imperative, and Materia Lucida is the
consciousness of the cosmic rays.
You are right in terming Materia Lucida the great
Mother of the World.
You are right in calling Materia Lucida, Cosmic Love.

Verily, the Universe is woven with the yarn of Lucida and the
lever of Love.
Poor humanity alone has clothed itself in isolation, with
the veil of dark denial.

Infinity I, #52[5]

(The above sloka, a spiritual verse, has been chosen for the tone that it sets, that the belief in separation cuts the human soul off from the love and truth of life. The consciousness of the soul and of oneness is imperative. It restores the knowing that the whole Cosmos is imbued with the spirit of love.)

-----

[5] Helena Roerich (amanuensis to the Master Morya). Infinity I, is one of the many Agni Yoga Society books, H.R. authored.

vii

I

INTRODUCTION
(In The Masters' Words)

"The Universal Laws are higher manifested expressions of the One Superior Intelligence that is the Creator of all life and are applied in the Cosmos, as well as, on earth. These Laws are simply the modes of expression that govern the spiritual operation within God's divine creation and keep the mechanisms of this universe working in divine order, maintaining total unification. In doing so, the Laws express the Will of God and lead to the manifestation of divine Purpose throughout His many universes. These Laws, supporting constancy since the beginning of all creation, ordain and nurture the Divine Plan and responsibly work in cooperation with one another to sustain harmony among all universal existences. This is called divine Wisdom operated by divine Love.

All creation is governed by law. The principles that operate in the outer universe, discoverable by scientists, are called natural laws. But there are subtler laws that rule the hidden spiritual planes and the inner realm of consciousness. Contained within these laws (or conditions) is the true nature of matter. Knowledge of these laws has an effect upon the mental urges. Mind is the builder. Stay in full mindfulness of the application of Universal Law as related to self and to others, and know that in love all life is given, in love all things move.

The Universal Laws are life impulses that provide a way of existence or activity, for all universes operate within a divine geometrical, mathematical and scientific perfection based on spiritual laws and principles. In fact, since the beginning of its creation the earth has been governed by the long array of Universal Laws just as other planetary bodies and star systems have. Scientists have been able to attain only a partial understanding of these Laws in the past because their understanding has been based solely on scientific theory which excluded the primal spiritual Divine Source, namely the acknowledgement of the Creator's involvement. This can be seen, for instance, in the example of the 'Big Bang' theory. With or without belief in God's divine system, the Laws are accurate and perfect and allow for no deviation. There is neither avoiding nor denying them for the Laws will always govern and control all that happens in time and space; thus no abnormalities can ever deter the functioning of this system.

A new divine order of creation is beginning to appear on the horizon, which will give humanity new hope and the potential of raising the human expression into pure joy, brotherly love, and harmony. These Laws will be the necessary tools by which humanity can be propelled into a higher vibratory level of existence and become soul-infused personalities in the future.

In order to integrate fully the concepts of spiritual initiation, or evolution in consciousness, the individual must come to a greater understanding of these spiritual Laws and apply them now in this present day. To reclaim one's power, spiritual and otherwise, and bring peace and balance into one's life, the individual must choose to live righteously in accordance with these Laws. By incorporating the Laws into daily life, meditation, and healing practice, humanity will eventually witness an unfoldment of greater serenity, intelligence and wisdom.

Until now most of the human race has had little experience in understanding their lives in terms of the Universal Laws, and unfortunately, because of their resistance to these Laws, or the lack of conscious knowledge thereof, their lives have resulted in painful self-infliction and suffering.

The Universal Laws are occult and basic, scientific and superior, and are the underlying foundation for the gifts of mastery here on earth. All the Great Ones within the planetary Spiritual Hierarchy and of the Cosmos adhere obediently to these Laws by the use of Their own will because They understand that the Laws are the backbone of the Divine Wisdom and the One Intelligent Life.

Today there are spiritual aspirants and disciples who are also choosing of free will to follow the spiral of higher evolution and are striving to implement these Laws effectively and creatively. These spiritually awakened ones, in turn, will be the pioneers who will show others how to live a new dimensional existence in the coming new era; for Universal Law is not only one of the fundamental ideals that will govern the New Age, but is truly a gateway to a higher dimensional consciousness and a pathway to understanding cosmic intelligence."
-Master Morya (Letter 1994)

"At the center of the Universe is the generation point of all energy. As we are conscious in the center of our being, so we are. From this Source of Central Force all the Laws of the Universe become manifest." -Master KH (Letter 2001)

II
HIGHER LAWS OF SPIRIT

1. LAW OF LOVE, ATTRACTION OR BALANCE

The greatest law in our solar system is the Law of Love. It is the great law that governs the soul. In its simplest form, the Law of Love is that law which places the welfare, concern and feeling for others above self. This is the great law that governs the soul aspect and is the one law that must manifest while all other laws seek to encourage and support. The divine quality that our Solar Logos, the great ensouling life of our Sun and its solar system seeks to express and demonstrate is: Love-Wisdom.

More scientifically, it is the law that governs by balance that which is produced by the rhythmic relationship or exchange between the negative pole of form and the positive pole of spirit. The energy of love draws the material of form back to its original sources before rebuilding it according to the Law of Cycles and Rhythm.

As more of humanity awakens to the soul,

the balancing quality of love will flow more freely into the world, finding receptive hearts and minds to respond and give back the love they have received. It is through unequal give and take that balance is lost.

Love is "the trinity of divine qualities: truth, goodness and beauty, of which the heart is the great detector. For those in humanity who are awakening to the soul, the heart exerts a magnetic attraction to divine love. For those who are attracted to the opposite qualities, there remains a gulf between the unredeemed personality and the soul."[6]

The Divine Love of God is a presence that fills the universe. It is the matrix of the universe and the nucleus – the magnetic cohesive force around which matter is drawn to create all form.

The ultimate goal of our Solar Logos is to actualize divine love through the Law of Love in the solar system. In Alice Bailey's Treatise on Cosmic Fire, p.1167, we are told that the Law of Love is controlled by a greater cosmic law, called the Law of Akasha, which is the principle of intelligence, potentially found in substance. The Law of Akasha will affect humanity when the Law of Love is in demonstration.

Attraction is the unifying bonding principle of the Creator's universe. The Law of Love or Attraction, is the intimate connection with all forces that you associate with as "good". If the cosmic significance of love could be realized, people would see in love its highest function,—the awakening of all the highest qualities of being and creative abilities. Precisely this awakening is the chief purpose and the true keynote of love.

Everything is created by thought. But for the fulfillment of any thought form to manifest, both the masculine and feminine principles must be unified and balanced by love. This law works to create outer circumstances that reflect inner states of consciousness. It works in a way that promotes the advancement of souls that seek to assimilate light and radiate light to others. In addition, bodies of finer, lighter substance can interact with higher realms of light.

The Law of Love is the force that denies evil a place in the world, yet does not resists it. Love offers the path of least resistance by cherishing, nurturing and protecting what is Good, True and Beautiful. Resisting evil only strengthens it. Christ demonstrated: "Resist not evil. Expose it, yes." Separative thinking does not exist in the soul and higher planes of consciousness, but does exist on physical, emotional and mental levels. Light reveals evil and light transforms it. Evil can never reveal light, nor create anything new.

This is why, until the soul and personality are integrated, the man cannot make an or sound use of the mind. The words sane/sound are chosen carefully. They connote a mind free of illusion and glamour.

A very high point of mental development is when the intuition, the spiritual organ for the direct perception of truth, is beginning to show itself. What always accompanies the intuition is the quality of love, the realization of oneness—a realization of unity with one's own indwelling God, with all humanity, with all souls in all forms of nature and with the universal soul.

Love is the driving motive for manifestation, and love keeps all in orderly

---

[6] 10 September 2020, Letter: "date-month-year, Letter" or "Letter-year" refers to a communication from the Fifth Kingdom. Two of the co-authors have worked in several group experiments, each with an amanuensis.

sequence; love carries all on the path of return to the bosom of the Creator, and love ultimately perfects all that is in manifestation. The Masters emphasize that the way to work with Love is through harmlessness. "Harmlessness dissolves obstructions to the free flow of Love. The expression of goodwill in the world is an indication that the the spirit of love is alive and well. The light of the collective human soul is becoming a powerful magnet for the greater light embodied by the Christ and the spiritual Hierarchy. There will come a point when the force of attraction will be so strong that nothing can keep the Christ and His spiritual Companions from returning to the world of humanity."[7]

When the Law of Attraction orchestrates the major currents of human activity, it will impel the quest for self-perfection. Love builds the forms that cradle the inner hidden life, and is also the cause behind the disruption of the forms, and their utter shattering, so that life may continue to progress. Love is the manifesting urge that propels the evolving consciousness onwards to its goal.

Love works through the will of the Creator in the rearing of the soul that harbors the spirit, and love works through the soul for the full and powerful revelation of the unity underlying all forms. Love is the way of union with God. It brings the human ego preoccupied with the pursuit of money and materiality, into balance with the soul. Love works through any consciousness that supports the balance of the universe. The will of our Solar Logos is to evolve the system in its outer form, in the fullest

measure and expression of this law.

The 20th century philosopher and alchemist R.A. Schwaller deLubicz said of the wisdom of Ancient Egypt that: "To be of the wise is to want to give and to be able to give. ..."To draw from the inexhaustible source and give that food to those who are hungry and thirsty."[8] It was divinely revealed to Walter Russell, the artist-philosopher and author of The Secret of Light, while in a higher state of consciousness, that the Law of Love is fulfilled through the one universal principle of rhythmic-balanced-interchange. From that revelation, he stated that "Rhythm" is the heartbeat of the universe, birth-rebirth. "Balance" is the equilibrium between the pairs of opposites, which holds the the sun in its orbit around the Milky Way galaxy, and "Interchange" is the exchange of the pairs of opposites through their giving and re-giving. Love is based on the principles of rhythm, balance and interchange.

The student who has received the guidance of a Teacher gives back the love received, not just through service, but by applying the Teacher's guidance. Imbalance occurs when there is not a reciprocation, when there is no re-giving, but receiving.

In giving, one attains. In giving, one acquires. In giving, love becomes the fulfillment of desire, guided and directed in the ways that bring the more perfect knowledge of oneself.

Love is Life and Light and when a soul goes back, and merges with the God Source, in some infinitesimal but profound way, that soul expands the Mind of God and enriches the One Life.

The soul always points out the best and

---

[7] 31 Oct. 2021, Letter

[8] Nature Word, p.134

most perfect way, and it is up to us to listen and choose, or reject what we hear. God does not blame, but patiently tries again to show the perfect way, the loving way. All of creation is pushing forward. We are always becoming, and yet one's divine identity always remains!

"The divine universe was created by energy as a means of expanding itself into matter. From the metaphysical perspective, this was the very first act of equilibrium, the balancing of spiritual energy with matter. In essence, it could be said that balance is the key that unlocks the secrets of the universe. For this reason, the contemplation of balance in personal and group life relationships, and in world service is most appropriate".[9]

The Law of Magnetism, referred to in the books of Alice A. Bailey is a subsidiary of the Law of Love, and produces a union of the personality and the soul. Love fulfills its own law, consummates the work of the Creator, and reveals the magnetic and radiant presence of Christ within the human soul. Love is a gathering of light into Light.

Love is always seeking an entrance into the human kingdom through which to pour itself out unconditionally. Love causes every vibration of creation to surge forward, carrying all along its path, and bringing all into perfect manifestation. Love is the life-giving force that allows spiritual alchemy to elevate matter to the heavens. Yet, love honors free will and every personality the soul has been, has had the freedom to create and develop. This is an important point to remember. Love is the unifying principle that maintains the universe as a unity and every form in it, and Love is the lever that keeps all

its operations moving in harmony and regularity, always honoring free will.

In the new era, all will be accountable for how they use the energies of love and this will include an evaluation of past lives by each individual from the perspective of the soul. When an individual is ready, past life reviews under the divine supervision of Masters will bring about healing, balance, a sound understanding of karma and a gain in wisdom.

Letting go of blame and judgment, will be one of the results of understanding the Law of Karma and the review of past lives. It will clarify the reasons for accepting accountability and taking responsibility.

Accepting accountability and responsibility will begin to "seal the door where evil dwells" and go on to purify the karmic remnants of humanly misqualified energy on the astral plane. This is so, so that humanity can understand the field of life of the soul and the universe.

The new age will be the age of the soul, the age of light and will also be known as the age of the Holy Spirit. The Holy Spirit is also known as the Shekina or "presence of God", a sacred name for the Holy Spirit. Loving one another as oneself is what opens the flow from the Holy Spirit.

The Shekina, a Hebrew word for the Holy Spirit, is the sustaining power of all-encompassing Love through the work of the Christ and the holy presence of God. It is the Shekina, that thwarts those wills that would attempt to interfere with the divine plan and purpose of God.

The Holy Spirit will bring the presence of God into manifestation, allowing many prepared souls the experience of the

---

[9] 29 December 2014, Letter

Shekina. To experience God's presence in all forms will bring a true understanding of this divine feminine principle. It is the presence of God that will solidify the relationship between the three planetary centers: Shamballa, Hierarch and Humanity. The increased activity of the Law of Love in the new age will restore the feminine principle and its presence in the world.

On the level of the soul, the Shekina is the creative expression of the individualized spirit of man. In the world of nature, it is the creative activity of intelligence, resulting in the beautiful splendor of natural forms.

The individualized spirit of man is the divine self, not to be confused with the soul or higher self. The divine self is the highest aspect of divinity called the Monad which expresses the will of God, while the soul expresses the love of God through the consciousness of the soul and the light of God through the soul-infused personality. The three, the personality, soul and monad are in essence one, but for purposes of manifestation, express as a trinity.

The Shekina is responsible for the sheaths or bodies of man's individualized spirit. In order for the man's individualized spirit to experience life in all its forms, it needs these the bodies of the soul and personality. All bodies are made of energy at different rates of vibration and consciousness determines the form.

There is a symbol, in the archives of the Masters, of the Shekina. It is a woman seated in the center of a blazing sun, personifying the universal creative power to be used by the Sons of Righteousness to balance, purify and uplift creation worlds in need of redemption,

regeneration and resurrection. It is the creative feminine principle that operates in balance with divine love and divine will. The Shekina is the magnetic force of divine love as the presence of God, that permeates humanity, drawing humankind back to the Godhood through the balance of opposites.

Only through a consciousness which realizes that duality is an expression of unity can the Shekina or Holy Spirit flow. The Shekina endowed spiritual authority upon the apostles through the blessing of Christ's love, as it filled them with the spirit of Love and Truth. In the new era, the feminine and masculine principles will be balanced as the soul is exposed to the radiance of the Christ and the Shekina. The true meaning of this law is grasped through the experience of the Shekina, the Presence of God.

A law subordinate to the Law of Love or Attraction which brought forth the light of mind in the early stages of human evolution, is the Law of the Lotus[10]. Its effects are those of association, form building, adaption of form to life and soul unfoldment. Using the Law of Analogy which gives all of life's expressions and kingdoms their linking correspondences, the Law of the Lotus relates spirit and matter as the rays of the sun relate to the plant kingdom.

The perfect Mind of God used this law to create every atom, every solar system, every human being. Therefore, no one can expect a response from Deity, if they violate the divine Law of Love. It is only through selfless love and love of God, that God responds within you. The Masters say, one must build up a reservoir of response. There must be selfless reciprocation. There has to

---

[10] One of eleven subordinate laws to the Law of Attraction, which will be revealed as human consciousness becomes established in the new earth. A general outline of them can be found in A Treatise On Cosmic Fire, by Alice A. Bailey, starting on p. 1166.

be a selfless giving so that there can be a re-giving from God. This is how the law works.

If a person were to think gratitude, admiration and appreciation for every cell in his/her body, he/she would be surprised at his/her well-being. God sees everything from each person's individual point of view and understands and responds according to their actions.

The soul's will is God's will, for humanity to evolve in consciousness, to become aware of itself as the "image"[11] of God, a seed of divine spirit destined to germinate, mature and ripen into its divine potential. As consciousness evolves, as soul expression is perfected, and as soul and form blends, the Law of Love is carried out.

It may not be possible to fully explain the Law of Love, but it can guide our way, when beckoned by a selfless heart and a peaceful mind.

Genuine love and genuine good cannot be coerced. It can only exist where there is free will. Some believe that free will is the highest good. The Masters say "use it accordingly".

Love, is man's supreme desire for God. Man is God's supreme idea, and love is God's desire for man. The following verses from a spiritual Elder, express the truth and beauty of this law:

"Anoint the palm of thy hand and heart with
the golden elixir of the Master's essence.
Forever seek to soften the mind
with the Law of Stillness. Beckon the
obedient Law of Love to come forth to show thee
thy way"[12]

~
"Thy heart is adorned with the Beauty of
God's love. Love one another explicitly.
For this is the key to peace and
brotherhood."[13]

2. LAW OF CAUSE AND EFFECT OR KARMA

This is the natural principle of karma or cause and effect, and it complements the Law of Love. When it is understood that God is love, this law, like all universal laws, is seen as serving the greatest good. Acceptance of the higher laws of spirit requires trust and a willingness to accept responsibility for one's actions. Karma, a Sanskrit word, means that every cause has its effect; every effect has its cause.

Take decision for example. Is there a right or wrong choice? Arriving at a conscious decision is a question of awareness, not habit or conflicting desires. To arrive at awareness and conscious decision, the laws are nonjudgmental in that they allow everyone freedom of choice and direction. A conscious decision is made with clear vision.

It is the lack of clear vision free which is today holding up the final activity. The higher perception of the soul is not the same as that of the human being identified with the personality. Higher perception leads to right action and right choice in what is good for the whole and not choices or actions that benefit the self. Humanity is gradually coming to an understanding of perception that leads to right human affairs by focusing

---

[11] The words "made in the image" (Gen 1:26-31) means made of the same substance.

[12] Letters, 1995-1997

[13] 1994 - 1997, Letters

on what is just and good for the many, not just the few.

All activity in creation occurs according to the divine order of the Creator which allows for choice, including transgression. Chance or luck is but a name for a cause or effect not recognized. There are many levels of causation, but nothing escapes the Law. It is always at work with chains of cause and effect in all of life and manifestations, where light and darkness exist.

If a person was to follow each link in the chain of causation, he/she will be find that it has its beginning and end in the realm of emotions, mind, soul or spirit. It affects the throwing of dice on a gambling table or a rock slide that is caused by rain and wind. Each can be followed and understood by the consciousness that sees the bigger picture and realizes that all things follow the Law.

Karma, the great Law of merciful justice, not retribution, is what regulates the duration and qualities of each soul's incarnation. Karma is unknown to the majority of humanity. It adjusts wisely, intelligently the effect to the cause, tracing the latter back to its producer. When this law is consciously applied, desired results can be scientifically produced in a person's life by directing him or her along definite paths of causation. When the law is applied in an unconscious and haphazard manner, the effects could be potentially disastrous for the individual or group. So called "accidents" could occur without warning to those who toil through life without awareness.

The human concept of justice is ignorant of karmic history. Until true justice is manifested through awareness, loving understanding and forgiveness, the karmic imbalance remains. It is like 'kicking the can down the road,' or 'sweeping the problem under the rug'. The problem will continue to rear its ugly head until the nature of the cause is reconciled, for example either by goodwill and right human relations or awareness.

This Law and the Law of Reincarnation are closely connected to justice and requires the acceptance of truth. To reconcile or resolve a conflict that has been brewing for generations and even centuries requires accepting responsibility or accountability for the part played by those involved. The key to this is the understanding that the causes lie deep in the present lifetime and previous lifetimes.

Until the underlying causes, present and past, are fully exposed and acknowledged, change is temporary and nothing really changes. Once the underlying cause is acknowledged, genuine change is possible. The solution when embraced is that of self-transformation. Jesus said "Go and sin no more", and He meant by that to change oneself and one's actions, not to repeat them. Self- transformation is a force that karma cannot resist.

People are responsible for the very thoughts that they produce. Fearful thoughts prevents a person from thinking and acting as the higher self would prefer. The cause of fear is the result of ignorance or a lack of knowledge about God, Spirit or the Laws.

Spiritual knowledge should be the most important educational journey in a person's life. Christ spread the light and love of truth knowing that fearful thinking can only be removed through understanding the knowledge of God and the spiritual path of transformation.

All the so-called evils under the sun stem from not knowing God, one's true Self. In the slightest thought, action, or deed that a person performs, he or she sets in motion invisible chains of causation and effect that will vibrate from the mental plane through the entire cellular structure of the body, out into the environment, and into the cosmos. Finally, the vibrational energy returns to its originator with the return swing of the pendulum. All this in less time than the blink of an eye. Because there are many dimensions of reality in which causation can occur, we remain unaware of many reasons for effects.

By an understanding of the soul and the laws one can learn to operate as an attuned individual instead of an unconscious personality accumulating restrictive karma.

This is one the few laws that can be scientifically manipulated by the enlightened mind. The Law of Karma requires that every human desire find ultimate fulfillment. The Buddha taught that personal desire is limiting and is the chain that binds man to the wheel of rebirth, and therefore spread the light of higher knowledge and wisdom, to counter the tendencies of the ego.

When humanity finally grasps the wisdom of the phrase, "As you sow, so shall you reap," it will move from selfhood to fuller soul expression. Belief or trust in higher knowledge or wisdom, not blindly but through a developed awareness, leads one out of suffering and actions which have karmic consequences.

Thinking, without awareness does nothing to balance one's karma. The perpetrator who thinks his or her crime remains undetected, breathes a sigh of relief and tries to dismiss the episode from consciousness, is deluding only him or herself.

It will come as a shock to the majority of the race to discover that karmic debts eventually come due. Human life on Earth evolves according to karmic law.

There are lords of karma, celestial beings, that work with humanity. These celestial beings are ruled by a greater lord of karma on Sirius that governs the karma of our planet.

A soul of the earth curriculum can only be liberated from their power, by receiving the higher knowledge of balance, which is connected with Libra. This is an aspect of initiation or expansions of consciousness. As humanity reaches maturity, more on Libra and the lords of karma, through the medium of law, will be given.

It is said that Christ is the restorer of justice and righteousness (Romans 10:4; Matthew 5:17). Christ's role in the Piscean cycle as World Savior was to fulfill an evolutionary need that can be summed up in love and forgiveness. At the end of the Piscean cycle when this great Light returns, Christ will represent the authority of God's law, justifying the karmic ledgers and balance sheets of the old cycle. Those who can hear, will understand the close link between love and karma.

In the new era, He will be the World Teacher and will begin by initiating a process in which each individual soul becomes aware of the ledgers to be balanced and lessons to be learned in the book of life. Christ will thus initiate the education of humanity from a new plateau and humanity will no longer wander in the dark, unaware of the laws or the purpose to life.

This law is without sentiment and it **does not mean** 'an eye for an eye", which Jesus made clear regarding personal interactions. The Law of Karma balances the scales of justice on the soul's journey to perfection. As mentioned before, nothing that happens in life is accidental or coincidental. The word 'coincidence' is a veil for the workings of unseen forces that shape the events and destinies of souls. The term "synchronicity" is a better choice to describe the subtle workings of these forces.

For those souls who lack even a glimmer of light and who wish to remain at their present stage for the next cycle of evolutionary, the law is precise and exacting.

"As you do to others, it is will be done to you" are words of karmic wisdom that also hav to do with thought: "Karma is created, weighted, or alleviated by thought. Thoughts and inner motives weave the aura, the subtle energy field surrounding the form, which is a magnetic field that either attracts or repels possibilities, and which ripples out into the universe. In fact, thought and motive—these crucial factors of karma—are often overlooked. If they are overlooked, it is impossible to break out of the cycle of cause and effect. For everything is karma and everything is held by karma."[14]

In the new era, the liberation of the self from karmic debt will be the concern of all as challenges and limitations will be seen in the light of the soul. In this light, blame will be less common. Engaging in blame will be seen as ignorance of the law.

The non-blaming, wisdom of the Law holds that our burdens are perfect as they are, that the Universe honors all choices, and that with forgiveness conscious action can balance the scales of cause and effect. Forgiveness is not pardoning, but the sacrifice of giving up one's self for the good of others, the group and the whole. Forgiveness is a virtue that unfolds from within, from contact with the soul.

It is one thing to avoid harming others for fear of karmic consequences, and another to realize that we are all interconnected in a single web of life, and to know that when we harm another, we harm ourselves. When fully established in soul consciousness, harmlessness is quite another thing. It is experiencing the presence of love to the extent that it becomes impossible to harm another.

The soul completes its karma by being itself the source of redemption to the personality. Suffering is the result of separation and identification with the personality. When separation ends, suffering ends.

Suffering diminishes as the spiritual seeker progresses on the path and with it, separation. Once separation is recognized as illusion, the ability to produce a union between the higher self or soul and its lower aspect, the personality is easier.

When Jesus said: "My God, why hast thou forsaken me?", it expressed in words His profound ability to tap into the sum total of all the agony of separation that his attunement to God and all God's children had brought. He allowed that to wash over him as was crucified on the cross. This was possible because of His realization of complete oneness, that there is not and never has been any separation from God.

The soul is, at its core, is made of God-substance—divine spirit calling the soul back to itself. When the realization occurs that there was never any separation from God, the soul reclaims it Sonship and the need for reincarnation ends.

In light of the spiritual journey back to God, the story of Adam and Eve's expulsion from the Garden of Eden needs some

---

[14] Roerich, Helena. Letters vol. II (adapted)

clarification. Tempted, they ate from the Tree of Knowledge or the Tree of Good and Evil, which now made them duality-conscious, with the free will to choose between right and wrong, light and darkness and the wisdom that comes with it. Had they eaten from the Tree of Life they would have functioned as pure spiritual beings, knowing oneness and not separation. They would not have known the difference between good and evil.

As for those trapped in decades of acrimony and ill-will, nothing will change until consciousness changes, until there is inner transformation. It is necessary to recognize the layers of history that have been permeated by forced subjugation, exploitation, and barbaric cruelty. When parties to a conflict can acknowledge and accept responsibility for their culpability over a lifetime and across lifetimes, often lived in bodies belonging to the religion, nation, or race of the enemy, then this is the greatest hope for justice, forgiveness, and true peace. The world will change when this understanding comes about. This is genuine forgiveness.

The human courts of justice accumulate evidence to determine reasoned remedies in order to examine causes that can be traced through recent history. They are unaware of the underlying pattern of causation that weaves its way into the present through the operation of the laws of karma and reincarnation. Without this awareness, the judgements given will be partial, leaving deeper causes unidentified. These deeper causes, working out through spiritual laws that result in the balancing of karmic debts, hold the key to mutual forgiveness and true justice.

In the new era, humanity will live joyously and creatively, not through any imposition of law but through the expansion of consciousness and the spiritual instruction that will be given by the Christ and the Masters of the spiritual Hierarchy. As mentioned in the Introduction, humanity will understand that the medium of "the laws are the backbone of the divine wisdom and the one intelligent Life".

It is important to note that when humanity is ready, three subsidiary karmic laws will be given that deal with the life of the advanced soul, known as: the Law of Necessity, the Law of Liability and the Law of Transformation. This knowledge is not yet time.

Expressed in the following verses are words of karmic wisdom:

> "Within the eye of God
> lies the reflection of the beholder.
> Think well in all that the say and do.
> A reflection is mirrored only once."[15]

~

"The evils which devour men are of their choice and making. They seek afar the goodness whose source within they bear. O' God! Couldest Thou save them by opening their eyes? No! Tis for the humans of a race divine to discern Error and to see Truth. Observe My Laws, abstaining from the things which thy soul must reject, discerning them well. Let thy soul over the body reign, so that ascending into radiant Ether [the new earth], Midst the Immortals, thou shalt be thyself a God [a fully unfolded Soul]."
-Golden Verses of Pythagoras (adapted, brackets, authors)

---

[15] 1994 -1997, Letters

3. LAW OF REINCARNATION OR REBIRTH

This law conditions the form life and it is important to note the difference between how this law is now perceived and how it will be perceived in the new earth. Hitherto, rebirth was understood as the assuming of ancient obligations, a recovery of old relations, an opportunity for the paying of old indebtedness, a chance to make restitution, an awakening of deep-seated qualities such as empathy, the solution of revolting injustices and the explanation of that which conditions and shapes one's life. The term 'life' from this point of view means the rebirth of the soul into a new physical body.

In the new era of light, identification will shift to the soul. This will bring the recognition that a human being **is** a soul on a journey towards perfection with all that this implies. Each life will be seen as an opportunity for spiritual growth and the time between lives as a period of rest and assimilation of the life experiences.

In the new earth, because the basic platform of life will be on the etheric plane, a timeless plane where physical death will no longer exist and where the soul is recognized, the result will be a re-visioning of the purpose of life. The purpose of life will be to integrate spiritual light into the substance of the new etheric-physical human form.

In the new era, when a cycle of learning is completed, and its fruits are gathered in consciousness, a new round of experience will begin. This will cause rebirth to be seen as advancement from one stage to another, an unbroken chain of life cycles and as souls and their forms become closer in vibratory resonance, the result will be more continuity of consciousness. Progression will be measured in terms of light vibration and emergence into the light.

In the new era, the fear of death will no longer hover over humanity, for the definition of a life span will be fundamentally changed by the fact that time on the etheric plane will be experienced as a higher dimensional experience of mind-space and not as a linear duration as in physical space-time, if that can be understood. In addition, the human body will be made of a finer etheric substance that is not subject to the decay that a dense physical body is subject to. This will result in the outer form not dictating the time of physical birth or physical death.

Nonetheless, the Law of Rebirth is a universal Law. All life forms go through a cycle of birth, growth, death, and rebirth. How this is experienced depends on consciousness. This law, properly understood, can do much to solve the problems of sex, marriage and suicide. It creates a sense of responsibility and a person who treads more carefully on the path of life.

"When Christ reappears as the World Teacher, the scales of karma will be balanced and the heavy burden weighing on the heart of humanity will be lightened by His words of renewal and rebirth."[16] Living in alignment with higher law will be seen not as something to be chosen out of guilt or fear, but as natural. This will lead to a collective intention within humanity for life to be loving, just and good for all.

An understanding of this law will lead the soul to higher levels of light vibration. That

---

which keeps one in the cycle of death and rebirth will come to be rejected. The coming World Teacher will also inspire the willing acceptance of responsibility for self and others, born of responsiveness to the true needs of the many through service to the Plan for humanity and the purpose of our heavenly Father.

The following facts about reincarnation are numbered and build upon each other:

1. The Law of Reincarnation is a great Law of nature on our planet.

2. It is a process, established and continued under the Law of Evolution.

3. It is closely related to and conditioned by the Law of Cause and Effect.

4. It is a process of progressive development which enables men to progress from the grossest forms of unthinking materialism to a spiritual perfection and an intelligent perception which will enable a man to become a member of the Kingdom of God.

5. It accounts for the differences among men and, in connection with the Law of Cause and Effect, for the differences in circumstances and attitudes towards life.

6. It is the expression of the will aspect of the soul and is not the result of any choice of form; it is the soul in all forms that reincarnates, choosing and building appropriate physical, emotional and mental vehicles through which to learn.

7. The Law of Rebirth, as far as humanity is concerned, comes into operation upon the mental plane of thought. Incarnation is motivated and directed from and upon the mental plane by the soul and its helpers.

8. Souls incarnate in groups, cyclically, under the Law, and in order to achieve right relationship with God and with their fellow human beings.

9. Progressive unfoldment, under the Law of Rebirth, is largely conditioned by the mental principle: "As a man thinketh in his heart, so is he." (Proverbs 23:7)

10. Under this law, man slowly develops the mind, then the mind begins to control the emotional nature, and finally reveals to man the soul, its nature and environment.

11. At this point in his development, man begins to tread the Path of Return, and gradually after after many lifetimes, orients himself to the Kingdom of God.

12. When an individual has learned— through practical service and understanding, to ask nothing for the separate self, he then renounces the desire for life in the three worlds and is liberated from rebirth.

13. The individual is now group conscious, aware of the soul in all forms and has attained a measure of Christ-like perfection reaching "The measure of the stature of the fullness of the Christ." (Eph. IV.13.)

As etheric vision becomes more developed among the members of the human family, laws such as the Law of Rebirth and Law of Manifestation will be studied in relation to the building forces and intelligences of the Devic Kingdom. Imagine an etheric earth in which the intelligences of nature are cherished and loved, and where form is known for what it is—the vase for the life within. Then, imagine a world where form allows the radiance of God, His power and magnetism to be revealed, revealing all that there is of form, life, beauty and usefulness.

The teaching of reincarnation by the religious priesthood of the world has been close to zero. In the new era, academies of light will be established as bases for spiritual education. Had a spiritual understanding of this law been seriously grasped by humanity, it would have encouraged many to escape the the painful and unnecessary process of rebirth. In the new era, the effect of this law and the Law of Karma will be the victory over "death".

In the higher frequency of new earth this law will take on new meaning. Etheric-physical consciousness of the new human being will not experience a physical death, but a timeless transformation of both consciousness and form in terms of vibrational quality. Rebirth will be understood as eternal renewal into limitless living light and life, with continuity of consciousness, so to live in harmony with all who serve God's plan. Humanity's relationship with time will change dramatically.

When any organic form is in a state of decay, it is approaching the end of its life cycle. So is a civilization, a planet and a solar system. Form, governed by such laws as these, including the Law of Cycles and the Law of Evolution, is simply a statement of the truth regarding the impermanence of form and that form follows consciousness. This in no way diminishes the sacredness of the form or matter.

Earth is about to enter a new evolutionary realm of existence. To understand this as a transition, as a passage, is to break with the ancient fear around death. Death simply shows the transitory nature of physicality

and the need for form to adapt to the evolving, deathless consciousness.

This is the essential message of this law. When this message is grasped, death and rebirth take on an entirely different meaning, as the life of the personality or the form is perceived from the perspective of the indwelling life. The soul's journey in form, from death to immortality, brings to light many lessons this law has to teach. A spiritual Elder gives the following verse to ponder:

"Differentiate between
empathy and sympathy,
for the latter will keep thee chained
within the cycle of rebirth."[17]

4. LAW OF ANTITHESIS

Compassion is the antithesis of passion which is selfish and grasping; selflessness, the antithesis of self-centeredness, which is always self-absorbed and dispassion, the antithesis of emotional desire. Illumination is the antithesis of glamour. Enlightenment, full awareness of one's spiritual identity is the antithesis of ignorance. The forces of destructive materialism are the antithesis of the forces of light that support life. Antithesis, however, produces the balance that is always necessary for right conditions.

Antithesis produces spiritual tension, a reservoir of potential energy in the life of the spiritual seeker and groups of aspirants and disciples, which strengthens the will and provides a great releasing power. But it must be a tension brought about by right orientation, that of the soul. This requires a discriminating mind which frees one from

---

[17] 1994-1997, Letters

personality preoccupations which produce extension, the antithesis of this type of tension which focuses one's whole being on the Real for the purpose of directing energy from soul levels and higher.

In the life of a spiritual seeker on the path of soul growth, there comes a moment when a point of such intense brilliance appears in one's meditation that everything fades away. This is a sign the soul is approaching closer to the centre of pure being. This "fading away" of everything has been described as darkness. It is a light beyond light which is the very antithesis of darkness as darkness is conventionally understood. It is the intense dark-brilliance of the synthesis, a condition of non-duality, where all opposites have been resolved into an indescribable unity.

This stage of consciousness expansion holds a profound wisdom. From in the Teacher DK's writings in The Rays and The Initiations by Alice A. Bailey: "at the place of tension, and at that darkest point, let the group see a point of clear cold fire." It is into the potential of this place of tension and seeing, that Aquarian group activity will have the opportunity to move towards. This will probably accelerate everything regarding the planet's evolution.

A group point of tension attuned to the "point of clear cold fire" is capable of working with and releasing a powerful form of energy, free from any impurity, for the working out the Plan. This is type of group spiritual tension is as of yet, out of reach. It would be equivalent to science developing cold fusion energy or faster than light space travel, utilized for the working out of God's divine purpose.

Shamballa is the major spiritual center upon the planet. It holds a point of tension that expresses loving will of God, free from impurity. It is pure good. But it cannot yet be passed safely through humanity. It must be stepped down by the spiritual Hierarchy before it enters the world. Only through a group point of tension, can this form of Shamballa energy pass safely through humanity for the fulfillment of the Plan. It can be seen how this law is connected with group activity and Shamballa.

Humanity, through a resonant point of tension, then assumes the role of planetary mediator between the higher and lower kingdoms of Earth, transmitting the energy of Shamballa, intelligently guided by divine love. The mid to later stages of the Aquarian cycle may see this unfolding of group potential.

But, this law has another meaning and purpose. The Law of Antithesis as stated in Letters of Helena Roerich II is, "The worst brings the best. Who, therefore, of the valiant toilers of the spirit, will not accept the full chalice? In the Teaching, acceptance of the full chalice is also advised, and we shall not deviate from this Advice. Let us not think that Christ, this Great Spirit, did not know what was destined for him. To each bearer of the achievement a full chalice is offered, and he himself chooses whether he wishes to accept it in its entirety or only a portion of it." It is a law that allows us to respond to the needs of the group and the whole.

This law is closely related to Gandhi's philosophy of "holding firmly to truth"; in Jesus' actions of cleansing the Temple and in his accepting the cup of physical death and suffering, he fearlessly held fast to the truth. The framework of non-resistance is not one of passivity but is a dynamic radiation of the inner self, the soul; it is the ability to think and act with pure reason or sound-mind, leaving the individual free (in the highest sense of the word "free") to think and act in oneness with the Mind and Will of God.

Helena Roerich shares her understanding of the meaning of this law in a response to a fellow student's letter: "Having suffered a deep spiritual disillusionment on my path, I have lost will and faith. Nevertheless, I still wait for the Teacher!" But if you wait, that means you have hope; therefore, faith is not yet lost, and this is most essential. Thus, let us go over your disappointments together and transmute them into accumulation of the great life experience, in the furnace of which our spiritual essence is conceived and strengthened. No theoretical knowledge, no philosophy can give you spirituality; only by drinking the cup of life's poison, with all its illusions, can we accumulate the Chalice of Amrita. And so, I would like you to establish a clear point of view toward all disappointments. Should one be terrified by the destruction of illusions? Each broken illusion is another step of knowledge. True knowledge is austere, as is the spiritual path, and only the spiritually strong can hope to approach the path of accelerated spiritual development. Moreover, this path can never be eased, since only suffering, only personal tension can transmute our energies and give them the necessary balance. But blessed is he whose heart is aflame with the exaltation of heroic achievement; supernal joy becomes his lot. Thus, kindle all the fires of your heart, and exaltation of the spirit will be yours."[18]

Accepting the chalice, as Christ, Buddha and many of the enlightened Ones have, will always bring about the best manifestations of labor. The Masters do not waste energy on a student's idleness or the feeding of

trepidation. The understanding, right use and mastery of this law leads to the courage to assert truth, break through the walls of resistance, pierce through the veils of maya and humanity, serve as a conscious planetary mediator.

5. LAW OF ALIGNMENT

This is not about personality alignment with the soul but living in right relationship with the higher laws that will replace the current societal and man-made laws in the new era. The alignment with higher law will basically come from the proximity of the spiritual Hierarchy and the Christ to humanity, which will stimulate the awakening of the soul.

"Social reorganization and economic reform must emanate from the awakening consciousness of man. One cannot legislate or lay down rules that will govern man when under a spell of hypnosis. A people's thoughts and motives cannot be organized until they conform to each other. It is in this realm that all differences arise. One person is selfish, another is unselfish. One is successful and another is a failure. One has unusual strength and ability, while another is weak and incapable. One thinks only of his material welfare and another thinks only of his spiritual welfare as entirely divorced from his outer nature. How can such diverging thoughts and feelings be organized into a harmonious whole? Only in a human being's innermost nature is there identification with others in thought and motive and only through bringing out what is within can there be peace and harmony in the earth." These are the words of Baird T. Spalding, who visited the Far East to study the teachings of

---

[18] Letters of Helena Roerich II

the Masters. He shared his experience in his book serie: Life and Teachings of the Masters of the Far East.

At the highest levels of consciousness there is Ultimate Truth—the principle upon which the entire universe and reality is based. When any law is corrupted by the absence of Truth, the result is disorder and decay. This has occurred on Earth to the extent that laws of nature have been subverted by humanity, with dire consequences for planetary life.

The world is full of the many versions of truth that compete to occupy human minds. The way to discover whether to believe an idea or a theory is to co-measure it with the intuitive perceptions of the heart.

The mind alone cannot be relied upon to separate truth from illusion. "The discerner of truth is the heart, for the heart is the portal to the down-pouring light of the soul that penetrates the mind with its wisdom. How does your heart respond when you land upon a statement of truth? Is there an energy flow that charges the cells of the body with light? Is there a sense of well-being that flows from the soul's registering of Truth?"[19]

Failure and the fear of failure when seen in their true light are karmic teachers of alignment. Even the best student, the highest initiate and Master has failed, for everyone has failed. Truly, there is no failure, only a measure of alignment. We learn through failure is a well known truth.

Trust comes from an inner knowing of what is true. It must be asked of any law—is this a law we want to apply to all people and would it create a world in which everyone is treated with dignity and respect? The philosopher Immanuel Kant is quoted as

saying: "Live your life as if every act were to become a universal law." Before you act, ask yourself: "Would I want my action to be a cosmic law?"

It is alignment with the soul and action, which flows from this alignment, which will transform the earth into a sacred planet, where divinity is recognized in every form.

"The power of the Soul pours like a steady current through our lives. May that power strengthen our will to serve.

The light of the Soul streams forth like a beacon upon our way. May this Light guide our steps.

The Love of the Soul wells up within our hearts. May this love pour forth to all we meet and be the cornerstone upon which we live. The Joy of the Soul irradiates our lives to lighten the burden of others. May we radiate joy to all Life upon the Earth.

The Will of the Soul becomes our will. We know no other. That Will is love and peace. May we play our part in the world with courage and strength.

The reflection of God's Presence is the Presence of our Soul. We walk with God by night and day. May we recognize divinity in every form."

- Gnostic Hymn (adapted)

6. LAW OF PERFECTION

This is a law which concerns the *process* of perfection. The Law of Rebirth is under this law. It must be remembered, that it is the mind of humanity, enlightened by the soul

---

and living in alignment with the higher laws, in cooperation with the Kingdom of Souls, that will transform the world.

Up to now this law has been concerned with the soul's chosen design for itself and the perfection of the soul's physical, emotional and mental bodies. In the new era, this law will be more concerned with consciousness, group activity and embodying the essential qualities of the soul. This law now extends its influence to include the path from selfhood to mastery through soul or group consciousness. Only through conscious human cooperation with the Kingdom of God, can Christ's vision of divine possibility for humanity demonstrate: "Be ye perfect as your Father in heaven is perfect." The Law of Perfection governs the entire process of perfection from that of an atom to that of a a Logos, calling forth imperfection to be transmuted.

In the past, the method of human perfection was the constant return of incarnating souls to the school of life on Earth. This time, when the Christ returns, new methods will be used, for earth and humanity will no longer be limited by the limitations of the third dimension. A case in point will be changes to the process and frequency of reincarnation. In an earth which exists outside the boundaries of the third dimension, Time as then and now, and Space as here and there, will no longer be an obstacle, allowing the soul more freedom in its progress toward spiritual perfection.

Through his own self-perfecting, the man Jesus was transfigured and gave to the world an expression of a new divine aspect, that of love based on realizing the oneness of all life in the universe through his identification with God, the Father and God as Love.

The Gnostic teachings from the words of the risen Jesus as the Christ, describes the nature of perfection: "There is one unutterable, illimitable, inconceivable, invisible perfection, the irreducible, unchangeable One that existed within itself, in its own eternal being, prior to anything else coming into being. The One from itself divided into two without changing, into Spirit-Father and Matter-Mother, a new Oneness which was Two but not Two. The One became the Many—the eternally existent All, but as long as the All remained in the Father's thought, the All in its part did not know the Depth of Him in which they found themselves.

"The One Perfection, greater than perfect, divided and made All and brought forth the All into being, but the All was not made perfect from the beginning. There is One Perfection, though the perfection within every member of the All is awaiting their becoming conscious of it. In other words, the All existed with the Father but did not exist for themselves. The kind of existence the All had was like a seed or that of an embryo.

"For that reason the Father had also thought in advance that they should exist not only for himself but for themselves—that they should remain in his thought as mental substance, but also exist for themselves that they might understand what kind of Father they have. They understood that the Father existed and they desired to find out who the existing one might be. The Father being good and perfect granted they should come into being for themselves also.

"The Father's Plan was that the All be granted to come into being for themselves and gracefully allow them to understand who the One Who Is is, to consciously know themselves as eternally perfect, who having come into being, into Mother-Matter, in order to consciously know who the Father, the One Who Is is"[20]

The words of the Christ: "Be ye perfect..." and the words of the Gnostic teaching above, talks about the process of perfection the All goes through. In Cosmic Whisperings, a very recent transmission of illumined guidance, the following words on the process of perfection and not perfection itself, are restated for these times: "To move into the next plane of evolution does not require perfection; that would be to miss the point of unfolding stages of evolution through which the human being advances toward self- perfection and self-transcendence. What is required is the ardent desire for a world of justice and peace where humanity can fulfill its divine potential and enter the Kingdom of Souls responsible for the further evolution of Earth."-atreeoflight.org/resources/star

From the point of view of the beginning disciple, one who is committed to the path, or the intermediate disciple, one who is committed to undergoing the disciplines of treading the path of transformation, a relative perfection comes about when the etheric energy centers or chakras of the body, have been purified for the entrance of the transfiguring light of Spirit. This takes patience, hard work, commitment to the path of selfless service and trust in illumined guidance. Anotherwords, a degree of spiritual maturity coupled with compassion and simplicity.

Taking pride in one's mental development or overestimating one's mental powers, or

boasting about the number of years one has studied, hinders the perfection process. "Every step toward self-perfection serves the advancement of the whole group. Thus, it is asked the work be taken seriously of mustering the will to more fully embody the essential qualities of the soul."[21]

The practice of simplicity quickens the perfection process. Non can imagine a more simpler life being led than that of the Christ or the Buddha. From the viewpoint of illumined guidance, simplicity is freedom from the glamour and complexity of the mind or ego. It is a love that asks nothing in return. It is one-pointedness when concentrating on a particular task. When one's life becomes the path and the path becomes one's life, one has achieved the simplicity of the soul.

The Teacher DK says in Discipleship in the New Age (vol. II), "Simplicity connotes the blueprint [of perfection] which substands the outer structure of creation, of living, of loving and of service, and this is true of a solar system, a planet, humanity or the individual."

Regarding compassion, there is a story about Buddha that believing that he had attained the final stage of perfection, was about to abandon existence in finite space and time, to abandon all sorrow and suffering for the pure being of universal and eternal bliss, until he realized: "The unique perfection of myself I dreamed, the perfection of my own character and personality is but imperfection while one other being—one single gnat—still suffers imperfection of its identical kind. No being may reach bliss alone: all must reach it

---

together, and that, the unique bliss proper to each. For am I not in every other being and is not every other being in me?"

The above story of the Buddha's quest for perfect enlightenment should help to revise the conventional understanding of perfection. Perfection is the substrate of existence, the essence of Buddha nature and Christ consciousness. This implies that perfection is not an end goal to be pursued but rather an absolute in which all living beings can identify with, within and without, according to one's divine potential and desire to find it.

The Christ saw perfection within every sin and showed the way to perfection is through simplicity, love, service and self-transformation. In the new era, the Christ and the Masters, will show that there is no death, but that life continues for the individual soul, until the consciousness within the form reaches a stage of relative perfection—the goal of human existence.

"What constitutes perfection? In essence, it entails living in alignment with Higher Law. This is what will transform the human race and create a world that is new. It is from the aspiration of humanity to live in spiritual alignment that new laws will emerge. Evolving humanity, under guidance from the Hierarchy, will establish principles for spiritual living to which awakened souls, by their nature, will willingly adhere. There will be no need for external control or imposition. These will be laws that serve the Greatest Good."[22]

Master DK in Alice A. Bailey's book, A Treatise on the Seven Rays says: "Deity itself is on the road towards perfection." This is a humbling thought to ponder.

The process of perfection is also connected to Beauty and the path of Beauty. "The World is striving for the crowning perfection. The closest to perfection will be the path of Beauty. If one should take all distorted manifestations of life and line them up with Beauty one would find the Law of Perfection."[23] The consciousness of a soul-infused humanity will transform the world and when blended with that of the Kingdom of Souls, will bring about an evolutionary change in form—earth into a sacralized planet of radiant beauty, joy, benevolence and truth.

The earth is moving into a higher vibratory octave where creativity and beauty will take center stage as the vitalizer of a spiritual culture. An Elder of the 5th Kingdom says there are the four dimensions to the creation of beauty in the new era. They are the individual's ability to:

1. Create consciously in mental matter.
2. Think with pure reason.
3. Complete works of quality and excellence.
4. Evaluate.

These all require precision, scholarly effort, spiritual perception, accuracy and a firm grasp of the laws and rules which govern working with the energies of light, sound, color and the devic evolution. These are the "qualifications" along with love and purity that will distinguish those attracted by the path of beauty in the new era.

With the movement onto a higher level of spiritual existence comes the joyous responsibility to participate in the

---

[22] 25 Feb. 2021, Letter

[23] Fiery World III, (note: the Law of Being will come into manifestation in the far distant future.)

manifestation of heaven's perfection on earth.

In the new era, individual's will leave a legacy of some form for the benefit of the common good. "To not act as if you are beings beyond yourselves, but of acting as Self-realizing human beings on the Path toward perfection. This is what a soul on the path of living discipleship becomes and what the world needs to see. An individual living up to these words, expands into the grace of the higher self."[24]

The Aquarian cycle is moving the world to a point of precision and accuracy, where dedication and alignment with God's laws is necessary. The new training ground in the Age of Light is illumined thinking with loving understanding and creativity. This will allow all individuals to grow in the light of the soul and contribute to the enlightenment arising within the lotus of human consciousness.

Overdevelopment of the mind and disrespect of universal law leads to havoc. "All who would be of the New Age cannot break laws...I tell you, you cannot do this and remain in the presence of these New Age energies."[25] The expanding new life of the new earth will be supported by divine law, instruction and guidance from the World Teacher and His Masters which will provide the balance to mental development.

The longing and love of humanity for God comes from the "immovable perfection" of the Self that lives within the soul and this great law. Immovable perfection is one with love—the driving force of evolution. It is the perfection of God revealed to the one filled with love.

There are star systems within the galaxy that have attained a state of higher perfection, a condition in which there is no imperfection—no opposition of good by any evil force and function. One such star system being Sirius, where its Logos is identified with perfection on a cosmic level. Earth is fortunate that a stream of energy flows from one of the three stars of the Sirius system directly into the spiritual Hierarchy. This will become a more pronounced activity within the affairs of humanity in the new era.

The Christ and Masters of the spiritual Hierarchy are returning. They will guide humanity in the new era towards perfection. The Elders of the spiritual Hierarchy have achieved a state of perfect peace through alignment with divine Will. They have embodied the immovable perfection that exists within every human being and which is one of the greatest gifts of life from the Creator of All, for it allows all just men and women to be made perfect.

"I have come to teach you about what is, And what was, And what will be, In order for you to understand The invisible world, And the world that is visible, And the immovable perfection of humanity."
-Nag Hammadi Scrolls, Book of John

~

"The wise man is perfect in all wisdom"
-Nag Hammadi Scrolls, Book of Thomas

---

[24] 13 March 2021, Letter

[25] Revelation, Birth of a New Age by David Spangler, p. 67, a quote from the Lord of Civilization.

7. *LAW OF GOAL-FITNESS AND CO-MEASUREMENT*

This is the law that nature follows. It is coming into activity as humanity develops group consciousness. It works on developing harmonious action, the reconciling of free will with higher guidance, and works closely with the Law of Perfection in producing sound mind. Experience and example are the teachers of this law.

For goal-fitness to succeed it needs the right attitude of mind. For example, "I failed to observe" rather than "I do not remember"; "As yet I have failed to learn" rather than "I do not know".

It is a dual law, in that both goal-fitness and co-measurement must be developed as the basis of cooperation with the Fifth Kingdom. It involves an individual and members of a group having a truthful recognition of one's assets for service and personality decentralization.

This law adjusts the student's relationship to the Teacher. It will also bring about a realization of the true significance of the concept of the Teacher. In the teachings of Agni Yoga books by Helena Roerich, it states: "One should not bring to the concept of the Teacher expectations of anything supermundane. The Teacher is the One who gives the best advice for life. This practicality will embrace knowledge, creativity, and Infinity."

One of the best examples of goal-fitness is how the Teachers of the Fifth Kingdom adapt Themselves and the Plan to the needs of humanity, and how each of them are continually fitting themselves for greater service. This law involves adequacy to the path. Where the power of higher love functions, goal fitness is at work. Goal-fitness requires the discipline of commitment until the goal is realized. Goal-fitness is a continual process.

This will become a fixed idea in the minds of all men and women and will lead to the fulfillment of the Divine Plan. Humanity's role as an intermediary between the higher and lower kingdoms is nurtured by this law.

Divine purpose can only be contacted as the duality of soul and form is fused into a oneness. The form then, becomes the medium through which the Divine Plan can manifest. The Law of Goal-Fitness nurtures the Plan and brings humanity closer to understanding the nature of divine purpose.

This is the law that guides the wise handling and surmounting of every crisis large or small that confronts those on the path of ascent. Goal-fitness brings an appreciation of the goal of evolution and the nature of divine purpose.

Achievement of the eight gifts and qualities (see Ch. IV) and will aid the needed group activity in the new er is to produce works of usefulness and beauty for the good of humanity. "Wherein wilt thou affirm the measure of thy works? If thy deeds be useful to the world, then is their measure great. Wherein wilt though affirm the quality of thy works? If thy deeds benefit humanity then is their essence of good."[26]

When something exhibits goal-fitness, it expresses, simplicity, beauty and usefulness. Goal-fitness requires the courage to approach it fearlessly. The Teacher tell us to think of the courage of the bird that flies across the sea, although no one thinks to

---

consider the swallow as a hero. Nature is full of wonderful examples of goal-fitness, great and small.

This is the law that deals with the economy of force and adjusts all that concerns the material and spiritual evolution of the cosmos to the best possible advantage and with the least possible expenditure of force. It is the law that perfects each atom, each eternal period carrying all onward and upward and through, with the least possible effort, with the proper adjustment of equilibrium and with the necessary rate of rhythm.

The application of the teachings of the enlightened ones and higher law is the best type of goal-fitness training. All the Teachers follow the Law of Goal-Fitness and sometimes a Teacher waits centuries before giving a sacred mission.

The Teachers advise that the person who seeks to be a bridge of communication between conditions of chaos in the world and Those Who work for constructive ends and order, should utilize the eight gifts (see Ch. IV). Where goal-fitness is present, time will be economized, energy will be wisely distributed and excessive zeal will be eliminated.

Group activity in the new era will provide the best training ground for goal-fitness. As it states in the teachings of the Agni Yoga books by Helena Roerich, "It is right to remember that work with Us has but a single direction — that of co-measurement and goal-fitness." Goal-fitness reminds us that work is not demonstrated by words but by selfless action and wise cooperation.

Just as builder has to know how heavy a load the pillars of a house can bear, in a similar way, there must co-measurement in one's thought and expression. What a coworker expresses must correspond to what he/she thinks.

Another term for co-measurement or a sense of right proportion is what the Teachers of the Fifth Kingdom ask of their coworkers, and that is personality decentralization-the sacrifice of the lesser self to a higher reality; the willingness to align one's life to a greater life. Goal-fitness and co-measurement are two factors which determines the extent to which the presence of Divinity can enter one's life.

Goal-fitness knows no boundaries. The Teacher's generosity and achievements will be the student's inheritance. The Teachers's path will be the student's achievement. Goal-fitness makes possible the manifested succession of Teachers which glows as a string of interplanetary pearls. The Teachers of the Fifth Kingdom say: "Add also your own pearl".

8. *LAW OF DETACHMENT*

One of the most important laws associated with treading the spiritual path, the Law of Detachment, works through the principle of Divine Love. It is not a self-imposed egoistic indifference or lack of concern for people, events or things. By reorienting of the affairs of men and women to the life of the soul, the aspirant recognizes love as the soul in others. This enables the registration of suffering with wisdom. It must be remembered that rounds of suffering are like purifying fires that destroy the illusory walls of separation that have defined the human experience until now. "Such experiences testify to the force of love that underlies the cosmos and is the beating heart of the

Higher Worlds. A force that is now accessible to you as you tap into its flow." [27]

Let the love that underlies the cosmos serve as a healing balm as you pursue the path of purification and meet the wounds of the past with detachment. Love is the first step in achieving the common goal of man; the manifestation of brotherhood. It is first a recognition of those in one's immediate group, as souls.

Gradually all the connotations of a relationship based on a Christ-like love, seep into the consciousness. One experiences the greatest of all gifts, the richness and fullness of God's love in man.

One of the most important steps taken toward this goal is a type of dispassion necessary for the unfolding of the soul nature. Why? "It is difficult for the neophyte to be impersonal when spiritual unfoldment is concerned. Yet, the very earnestness of aspiration may serve as a hindrance, and one of the first things the neophyte has to learn is to go forward along the path, adhering to the rules, following the practices, employing the means and steadily fulfilling the law and at the same time to be occupied with the vision and with service and not with himself. It is so easy to be the victim of high desire and so busy with the reactions and emotions of the aspiring lower man that rapidly one is enmeshed afresh in the toils of the versatile psychic nature." [28] Intense preoccupation with one's own growth is a glamor. The cry is, "Tell me, tell me, then I will change" which is the antithesis of the attitude "Aid the work. Forget yourself. The world needs you."

As Christ and Buddha demonstrated, detachment from the personality or not-self brings about greater participation in life and helps to adapt to different realities. Identification with the soul leads to detachment from form. Self-centeredness had its usefulness. It served the unfoldment of the personality. The enlightened ones say not to hate the form or attachment to it, but to love and serve with detachment. There is no pain or agony for the selfless one who has attained liberation, who has sailed beyond all obstacles. The consequences of karma are most frequently the result of self-centered actions.

It is a shock to many people to discover the existence of a spiritual kingdom, having lived under the 'modern age' assumption that there is no Spirit and that there are no karmic consequences for one's actions — a result that comes from the lack of knowledge of Reality. The ignorance of the existence of higher spiritual realms has contributed greatly to the human suffering that has resulted. Detachment maintains mental equilibrium and clear thinking.

It is vanity to think that the practice of detachment has any value while attached to results or while not addressing old patterns of behavior. Detachment is not something learned from a book. It is a remembrance of one's Buddha or Christ nature, born of soul contact, meditation, service and the path of self-transformation. Mastery of this law is not only possible, it is essential.

---

[27] 6 Aug. 2020, Letter

[28] Light of the Soul, Alice A. Bailey

9. *LAW OF RESONANCE OR CONCORDANCE*

Resonance or concordance occurs when two or more connected objects or living organisms share the same vibrational frequency. These words are used interchangeably. When one object vibrates, it causes the other to mysteriously respond in similar vibration. The musical definition of consonance and the scientific definition of resonance are close but not completely accurate in describing the type of agreement or relationship this law expresses—being of one mind. Two objects or living organisms in resonance such as tuning forks or groups will potentially amplify and reinforce each other into greater harmonic unity or vibrational resonance.

In general, the consciousness of humanity has not evolved as the Hierarchy had hoped in the last two thousand years, despite all efforts. It is what has delayed the Christ's return and the externalization of the spiritual Hierarchy or Fifth Kingdom. There has never been a mandate imposed upon humanity until now. Our Planetary Logos is going through an initiation, at the same time the Shift is happening. This is affecting all life on the planet, including the spiritual Hierarchy. All these factors have mandated a raising of the vibrational frequency of human consciousness.

Christ appeared two thousand years with the message of self-transformation. It was to prepare humanity for entry into the new world of higher vibratory frequency. Everything in the universe is primed to function at a particular frequency. It is this law which holds the key to entry into the new earth.

For humanity, the key to understanding everything at this momentous choice-point is —consciousness. Raising one's vibrational frequency, vibrational resonance is the key to moving into the new earth.

The analogy of understanding from a spiritual perspective, mathematical operations, will shed some light on this law. Subtraction is one of the four mathematical operations, the others being addition, division and multiplication. Spiritually, each mathematical operation corresponds to a level of consciousness: Addition-physical; Subtraction-astral; Multiplication-lower mental; Division-higher mental. Pythagoras is purported to have said: "All is number."

To give an example, in the process of self-transformation, a person subtracts and divides, division having the same effect as subtraction, but on a higher level. Whenever a person is removing a glamor, an emotional obstacle or eliminating something which separates the personality from the soul, that person is actually developing the higher mental faculties via subtraction and division.

The universe was conceived in the Mind of God by creating a thought-form in consonance with its united meditation. As a human mind learns to resonate to the divine qualities of unity, goodness and love, the vibration of the physical, emotional and mental bodies are raised to a higher frequency of perfection. This is what Christ meant by "Be ye therefore perfect." Christ also said: "When two or more are gathered in my name..." which is related to the mathematical operation of multiplication.

Consonance to the forces of fear, anger, frustration and resistance to evolutionary flow, also amplifies those disturbances in the body-soul field, but in the opposite direction, lowering the vibration and cutting one off from the higher currents of Light.

When resonance occurs between the soul and personality, unity is achieved. The same is true for the 4th and 5th Kingdoms in nature. When there is enough of a vibrational frequency between Humanity and Hierarchy, a resonance will occur and an unprecedented unity will be achieved on a planetary scale.

It is a fact, that every soul is divine and therefore inherently resonant with spiritual realities. But first, it takes recognition on the part of a human being to create spiritual resonance. "Dwelling within such souls is a bright spark of recognition of the spiritual necessity for the Christ to return to the world at this time. Because of this evolutionary necessity, many souls are willing to put themselves through rigorous tests and trials along the path of ascent and willing to subject themselves to the fires of purification. It is because of this there are those willing to engage in an accelerated process of self-transformation for the goal-fitness needed to fulfill a specific role of carrying out a portion of the Plan as formulated by Masters of the spiritual hierarchy."[29]

A decision was made many eons ago, to introduce and implement the process of initiation on earth, a series of graded expansions of consciousness to accelerate the spiritual development of humanity which was lagging. It had worked on the planet Venus and due to its success there, was brought to earth.

Initiation requires a vibrational resonance of all the chakras of the body and this entails a Master - disciple relationship, which over time and lifetimes, provides an intensification of energy exchange between a disciple and Master, affecting the disciple's consciousness. "With such a consciousness, one may verily become a co-worker for the transformation of life."[30]

When people will come to understand the unnecessary need for rebirth, this law may be taken more seriously. The realization of this law will bring about the continuity of consciousness and great help from "above".

Consonance is harmonious and sympathetic vibration. It also refers to the harmony that exists between an individual's vibrations and the cosmic vibrations which results in creative tension for service—a consciousness wisely focused on constructive achievement, an activity that draws one forward in the direction of evolution. The soul uses creative tension in sounding forth its note stimulates the personality until finally the mind and heart become one with the soul's focussed meditation.

As more groups find themselves working with an inner Ashram, "it is accurate to use the term 'concordant soul' for a member in the group but not to confuse it with the term a 'group soul'. "It is incorrect to call the concordant soul a group soul. Some translations and commentaries have produced this confusion. Plato's conception of twin souls [resonance between souls] not only was closer to the truth but was expressed beautifully. Thus, the term group soul for an individual is replaced with the

---

term spiritual concordance."[31] A group soul, therefore is a group of spiritually concordant souls in which there is a unified vision in accord with the plan and purpose of the planetary Logos.

Arriving at spiritual resonance affirms soul identification and generates beneficial change. An individual awakening in soul identity, may find it necessary to disassociate from old relationships and discovers new ones. Spiritual resonance recognizes the existence of the inner seed of spirit and simultaneously the concept of outer change.

The cosmic vibrations now affecting our solar system are allowing matter to directly feel the stimulus of cosmic vibrations. The nature of these cosmic vibrations is setting up a resonant pattern in which "negative forces" cannot remain in, for any length of time due to the presence of their Light.

Higher Beings work with the Science of Light to activate planets with specific vibrational attunements, so that planets can be brought into resonance with higher evolutionary patterns. Evolution requires a great deal of coordination and cooperation. Without a directing divine will, divine law and the host of higher beings, the higher evolutionary progress of worlds would not be possible.

Though the word resonance was not in the vocabulary of Plato's time, he was referring to this law when he spoke of the likening of the unlike using the term "stereometry". He said a man who acquired this art, sanctifies not only himself but also the city and the age in which he lives.

Vibrational resonance allows a higher will to impress itself upon a lesser will until there

is a "likening". It is this law which deals with powerful energies in accordance with God's Divine Will and Purpose In the Agni Yoga book, 'Hierarchy', the Teacher says that without the human soul's contact with divinity, it is impossible to affirm the fiery creativity and love of the spiritual Hierarchy.

This law is closely linked to laws of perfection and enlightenment. "We learn to perfect ourselves in accordance with Christ's injunction, already mentioned and worth repeating: "Be ye therefore perfect." In this way the spiritual reality of which St. Paul speaks, "Christ in you, the hope of glory," is realized and can manifest itself in full. When a sufficient number of people have grasped this idea, the Christ life will blossom in the human kingdom."[32] Perhaps in St. Paul's statement above, He was speaking of this law as well as entry into the new earth.

*"How does one enter the new era?
The key lies in the resonance of vibratory frequency. Everything in the universe is primed to function at a particular frequency.*

Taking responsibility for one's thoughts, emotions and actions, puts the consciousness in resonance with the soul, and the vibration of every atom in one's being is raised.

It gradually dawns upon the mind that there exists a realm of souls and that Spirit permeates all lives with an all-embracing love.

For humanity, this awareness is the key to life in the new era. The resonant vibration to moving through the door opening to life in the new era is: Spirit infuses all forms with Love."

---

[31] Fiery World I (Agni Yoga books), brackets, authors.

[32] From Bethlehem to Calvary, Alice A. Bailey

-atreeoflight.org (see Cosmic Whisperings and the youtube video: At The Dawn of a New Era)

10. LAW OF SUBSTANCE

This is a law that will be found operating in a greater capacity in the new era when the Law of the Akasha (mentioned earlier in the Law of Love) which deals with the intelligence of substance is revealed in the future. It is important to explain what is meant by Substance.

Life and Substance are two aspects of the one energy at different rates of vibration. Life is positive (Masculine) and Substance is negative (Feminine). Life is activity in a potential state and Substance is static. Life is spirit. Substance is form or matter. Life is substance in its highest vibration. Substance is life in its lowest vibration. Inherent in substance is its counterpart, life, and vice versa.

Life and Substance are one and inseparable yet, manifest as two, for the purpose of creation. This is the nature of the number two. It is unity manifesting as duality, relationship and love. God, by dividing a fraction of Himself and remaining unchanged, manifested as two, for the purpose of creation. As mentioned earlier in the Prologue, "The divine universe was formed by living energy as a means to expand itself into matter."

Substance provides life with a field for manifestation. In the interaction of Life and Substance comes a third aspect- Consciousness or Soul, active energy. All three coexist as a Trinity and at the same time exist as a single unity. So, we have Life, Substance and Soul—the three in one, God in manifestation with Consciousness as the mediator between spirit and matter. Thus, from the perspective of divine cosmology, the mixing of the three together, simultaneously, triggers the cosmic drama, whose source is the Unbegotten Immutable One.

Consciousness is associated with the number Two, because it relates spirit and matter through the attractive power of of its own nature—Love. Love has the power to take duality, unite the two and, thus reveal and express the Oneness of God. The many world religions have names for perfected manifestations of Consciousness: Christ, Buddha, Vishnu, Krishna, Messiah, Imam Mahdi and Maitreya.

This law is presented because it is closely connected to humanity's evolving relationship with the Kingdom of Souls, its externalization, the Divine Plan and the realm of subtle energies. Since "form follows consciousness",[33] it is necessary to know of the methods by which subtle energies are used to achieve results.

It is a law that will become merged with the Law of Love. It is intimately connected with purpose of our Planetary Logos, the being who is the God or Divine Source of the life of Earth, and the Feminine principle which makes possible the intelligence of substance. "The thought of God brought the universe of energies into organized form. Spiritual Masters manipulate subtle energies in conformity with the Plan, which is the blueprint of the Purpose of God or a Logos. In the approach of the Hierarchy to humanity, centers for the directing of subtle energy will be found wherever a Master's Ashram is located in any part of the world.

---

[33] see The Law of Evolution

This is of profound significance as it will deal with modern science, working as it does with energies, being brought into cooperative association and relation with the Masters' externalized Ashram, knowing it for what it is—an entirely new departure."[34]

The laws that govern the life of the disciple and the Master are the same laws that govern all life and these laws deal with consciousness, energy and substance. Through a realization of the purpose of these laws, the energies they deal with, and their conscious judicious application, the disciple is able to use the divine storehouse wisely.

Entering the divine storehouse and keeping it replenished requires the knowledge of how to do this wisely and skillfully, so that the bountiful supply of Spirit is brought into contact with the need.

"It is only as a skillful use is made of the supply for the needs of the worker and the work that supply continues to pour in."[35] This law states that energies must be used skillfully according to spiritual need. Only when the door is unlocked by the spiritual need or demand is another higher door unlocked to allow the supply, otherwise the storehouse can be depleted.

As this process goes on between the groups and the externalized Ashrams of the Masters, the Plan unfolds. This is one of the ways, in the new earth, that vibratory frequency of the bodies that the soul wears will become lighter and less and like a veil hiding the indwelling soul. This is one of the laws that will bring divine inspiration to humanity.

11. LAW OF DEATH, DISINTEGRATION OR SACRIFICE

It may be difficult to equate death with sacrifice, but, when viewed deeply through the lens of the soul, it is the death of control by the personality or form. It is also freedom from the death experience and bondage of materiality through soul unfoldment and the help of higher consciousness Teachers.

As humanity leaves behind its separative existence and takes its rightful place alongside advanced beings of spiritual intelligence, it will understand that death is an illusion. Humanity's fear of death stems from identification with the physical body—a form that is subject to decay and destruction by the same physical forces that erode all things made of dense matter.

The Law of sacrifice and death is the controlling factor of the physical plane. It is a law that governs the gradual dissolution of concrete form and its sacrifice to the evolving life. It must be understood that death is really an illusion, but it exists to fulfill an evolutionary function, that of spiritual progress.

The destruction of the form, in order that the evolving indwelling life may progress, is one of the fundamental methods in evolution. This is the symbolic message of the crucifixion and the cross of matter, the fundamental Law of all group work, the governing principle which results in each human unit eventually becoming a resurrected son of God, living for the good of all.

---

[34] Externalization of the Hierarchy, Alice A. Bailey

[35] Letters On Occult Meditation, Alice A. Bailey

There is an initiatory experience in the life of an advanced soul when an inner electrical phenomenon occurs. The inner light irradiates with such force that it causes the subtle body of the soul to dissolve. This allows the soul-infused personality to form a unified relationship with its monad—the individualized, indivisible, indestructible divine spirit, the higher divine aspect of the soul.

It is this inner electrical phenomenon, an effect of the Law of Death, which dissolves the subtle body of the soul, allowing for the the monad and the (soul-infused) personality to merge. This is a higher fusion than that which occurred between the soul and the personality.

At long last the fullness of the Christ-principle within: "Christ in you the hope and glory" - Colossians I: 24-29, is achieved and the advanced human soul is no longer bound to rebirth. It seems paradoxical that the Law of Death leads to freedom from rebirth, but it is so.

The Law of Death or sacrifice is different from the soul life, Law of Sacrifice (see Ch. III). The former involves the destruction of the subtle body of the soul and sacrifice to the monad, while the latter involves selfless, unconditional giving.

The death of the physical form is both an illusion and an impersonal teacher of karma. As a result of the destruction of Atlantis it was necessary for humanity to learn that death, not only brought about by natural causes is also brought about by the misuse of the physical body, psychologically, by misapplied energy and by the deliberate deeds or actions of the man himself. Atlantis set the Law of Karma in motion.

The person who intentionally wrongs his fellow human beings through psychologically wrong attitudes and actions, does not realize he is committing suicide, just as a person who deliberately causes the death of his physical form through self-mutilation or suicide. The truth of this will become increasingly apparent.

There is a world of difference between those who choose to die by personality action and those who choose to die spiritually to the physical by treading the path of self-transformation. It is why, this law is also called the the Law of "those who choose to die". The symbol is a rosy cross with a golden bird hovering above it. It is a law that is be seen as compassionate and constructive.

A word should be mentioned here about the fear of death. How is it transcended as an illusion and as fear? By recognizing the reality of the Soul and identification with it. On the spiritual path, the fear of death gives way to the understanding that death is actually the continuation of life on higher planes of existence. Only the form aspect of life ends after it has served the purpose of the indwelling consciousness of the soul for a particular cycle of manifestation. The idea life ends with death is a mental obscuration created by form-identified thinking. The true nature of life is eternal, full and free, realized through all the experiences the soul in form acquires as it evolves. Why would the Creator make death total destruction?

"The consciousness of the new Earth is rooted in Life and fulfilling its higher potentials. Everything will change when it is understood that Life is Spirit—inextinguishable and unceasing. The future of humankind rests upon the realization that spirit infuses all living forms. Spirit is the creative force behind the whole of existence. Try to imagine being alive without the fear of death, and in its place the realization that when the form is outgrown the wearer will give it up for a period of rest before another form is taken on. There will be an underlying awareness permeating the human experience that the purpose of life is to enlighten Life in all its forms. Death will have an entirely different meaning as the purpose of life is perceived in the context of the soul's journey toward perfection."[36] It is recommended the above words be pondered and its vibration allowed to soak into the mind and heart. In the words of one of the Masters:

> *"Abide in the Oneness and*
> *listen to Thy Master's whisper.*
> *...Eternal life awaits thee."*[37]

12. LAW OF SUPPLY AND DEMAND

It is this law and its implementation through the enlightened guidance of wise and loving beings that will determine the standard of living in the new era of spiritual rather than material values. It works closely with the Law of Substance and the Law of Manifestation.

This law has nothing to do with the requests of the lower nature or materiality or the old ways of manifestation. It is a law which is implemented by the Fifth Kingdom.

When there is no longer a desire for the separate self, the clue to this great law is found. This law operates on the principle of justice and abundance for all. It will come into full swing when the world trend is towards spiritual living.

A spiritual request sets this law in motion. It can be expressed through prayer, imagery, ritual or whatever method, so long that it harms no one. A request that harms another, either in the process or in the result of the manifestation, is not of the divine and will carry a karmic debt.

Then there is the selfless or spiritual demand that this law seeks to address. How does it serve all of humanity or at least others besides myself? How can the Law of Supply and Demand be implemented so that there is justice for all and abundance for all? Is the demand worthy? Is it in accordance with the Plan?

In the new era, as consciousness expands and the soul matures, humanity will enter into creative cooperation with the spiritual Hierarchy in the implementation of this Law. This will bring about the right relationship to demand, supply and giving, and a better understanding of the Lives that guide humanity's progress and formulate the Plan.

An understanding of this law will bring an end to the exploitation of planetary resources. The inclusiveness of this law also benefits the progress and well-being of all forms of life on our planet.

Supply and demand from the perspective of this law, result from the interaction of forces on the etheric and higher levels of life. This requires the constant adaption of matter to these interacting forces and this the initiates and Masters do through the wise use of light, color and sound, and in working together with the devic kingdom.

In the past one could ask through prayer, visualization or affirmation which harmed no one, and benefited all involved. In the consciousness of the new era, one will reach a point where the need to ask is not

---

36 https://whenthesoulawakens.org/cosmic-whisperings-2010_399.html

37 1994-1997, Letter

necessary. It will be the consciousness of many, focused in the soul, that will call forth the perfect supply, not out of need but out of recognition of the spiritual demand that emanates from the Lives that guide humanity. A spiritual demand is selfless and soul-based whether it is an outer (humanity) or inner (spiritual Hierarchy) demand.

Those whose soul faculties allow them to work on the inner planes respond to the demand and when it reaches a certain level of tension, a cross is formed between humanity and the spiritual Hierarchy—a vortex or energy center is formed that allows for the flow of energy between the two. More and more, individuals and more recently groups are finding their way into this vortex and are able to act as conduits for the energetics of spiritual supply and demand.

By trusting in their guidance and cooperating with the enlightened beings who implement this law, groups become centers of distribution from which perfect supply will manifest to meet perfect need.

13. LAW OF GRAVITATION

This law is a subsidiary Law of the Law of Attraction, closely related to form and the form-soul relationship. This law can be puzzling and confusing to some. Of all the laws, it works in two ways. For example, with the 'force of gravitation',[38] science has found ways to isolate humans and objects from it in space exploration, not so from the Law of gravitation. Material science does not yet understand its spiritual aspect.

There are several aspects to the Law of Gravitation. As a force, it manifests as the power and the stronger urge that a more vital life can have upon the less vital, such as the power of the spirit of the Earth (the planetary entity, not the planetary Logos) to hold all physical forms to its body and prevent their "scattering." For the physical manifestation of a planet and the form-soul relationship of a human species to occur, both the objective force and subjective Law of Gravitation are required. It must be remembered that the spiritual principle is the origin of the physical law.

Gravitational force is due to the heavier vibration that material science calls mass, the greater accumulated force of the body of the planet itself. This "heavy" force acts upon the lowest or densest aspect of all physical forms. This is the force of gravity that physical science is familiar with.

The Law of Gravitation, here treated, is manifested in the response of the soul of all things and to the greater over-soul of the Great Spirit or God.

This law holds the potential for universal brotherhood, while relationship and spiritual progress manifests it. This last sentence conveys the meaning of Jesus' words: "Those who do the will of my Father, are my brothers."[39]

This law governs the relationship of a unit of life in form to its emanating source and is thus related to the intent of life units to find their way back home, to return to the registering source. One aspect of gravity attracts form, the other soul.

---

[38] The force of gravitation and the Law of Gravitation are one in principle but different in their natures. The force of gravitation is related to form and physical in nature. The Law of Gravitation is related to the soul and spiritual in nature.

[39] Matthew 12:46-50

A planetary Logos is the sum total of all the souls of a planet and represents the attraction of the Oversoul to all the souls on earth. At a certain stage in the spiritual journey the ardent seeker seeks to bring the soul into unity with the divine will of the planetary Logos. From this identification, the soul obtains a profound vision of divine life and power The relationship of the soul to the Oversoul is the cosmic equivalent of the part to the Whole.

This law affects the two lower forms of divine life in the human kingdom, the personality and the soul, but not the third or highest divine aspect of a human being - the individualized spirit or monad. It is this law that deals with the gravitational force emanating from the physical Sun which holds the planets in their orbits and the attraction of the planetary Logos to the Solar Logos.

The gravitational force of the Sun, emanating from its physical mass and the Solar Logos creates the awareness of the relationship between the lower self and the higher self or the personality and the soul.

Human beings, through the influence of spiritual light and love, become aware of their essential duality as personality and soul, and will eventually attain soul consciousness through self-transformation.

There is a final attractive force called called Synthesis which may be regarded as divine gravitational activity, due to the action of a higher law, the cosmic Law of Life or Synthesis, emanating from the Logos of the galaxy, the central spiritual Sun, the Sustainer of Life. This great central Sun acts upon the monad, the highest divine aspect of a human soul. This will not take effect in our solar system until the far distant future, when our Solar Logos reaches a certain evolutionary stage.

The manifestation of the soul is a goal of of our planetary Logos. Earth's sister planet, Venus, its Logos having manifested the soul on its planet, has reached a high point in her evolution and is assisting our planetary Logos, motivated by love. There are many other celestial beings in addition to the planetary Logos of Venus who are adding their quota of light to the earth and her planetary Logos. This law that nurtures the universal principles of brotherhood, sacrifice and service, and works closely with the next law.

14. *LAW OF MAGNETIC CONTROL*

The Law of Magnetic Control is slowly coming into focus. Through this law, the Christ Impulse, the great liberating and redemptive power of God, drives the souls of humanity to progress through the cycle of reincarnation back to union with Source. It is what impels the incarnated soul to undergo the learning process necessary to transcend the lower self, and find unity with all selves.

It was the Law of Magnetic Control that caused the fourth kingdom in nature, the human kingdom, to come into being, and it rules on the mental plane, just above the astral plane. It is also a law which govern our Solar Logos and is coming into greater activity as a result of the cosmic ray of harmony which brings harmony out of conflict and struggle, coming into activity in 2025. The significance of this law is that it relates the solar logos, the cosmic ray of harmony, humanity, translating into great potential for progress and spiritual transformation.

The intent of this law is to make the soul more magnetic to the personality. The higher etheric nature of the new earth and the new etheric-physical human bodies will also facilitate making the soul more magnetic to the outer etheric-physical form. The quest for beauty and truth will be an outcome of the Law of Magnetic Control.

Hidden in this law is also the control of the personality by the monad, not just the soul. To come under the Law of Magnetic Control is a testament to humanity's ability to spiritually progress by taking advantage of learning opportunity that incarnation offers. It is the love aspect of the soul and the mental faculty, illumined by the light of love, through which this law operates.

Evolution progresses through the Law of Vibration and vibratory levels of consciousness. There is the higher mental level, the level upon which the soul exists and where the personality experiences more soul consciousness. Just above the higher mental level is the Buddhic level where more highly evolved souls exist. On the higher mental and buddhic levels, the Law of Vibration transforms into the Law of Magnetic Control.

The Law of vibration on the plane of Buddhi, as the Law of Magnetic Control, manifests as the love-wisdom aspect and irradiates the souls on the higher mental level. When the soul evolves and reaches the level of Buddhi, is when the soul becomes both radiant and magnetic.

It is worth repeating, it is the soul that reincarnates through the personality and to reveal its divine nature in the world of form. When the personality, the incarnated soul, reaches a certain stage on the path of transformation, the Law of Magnetism kicks in.

Where it not for this law, human intellect would be able to progress spiritually. It is now necessary for humanity to understand that intellect alone is no longer enough. Intellect transformed by the light of love and truth is now required if humanity is to survive and continue its evolution.

It is this law on very physical levels as the Law of Vibration that makes every thought created act as a boomerang, creating a match that returns to the sender.

The Law of Magnetic Control allows a group to develop magnetic usefulness, drawing in others through the radiant love of the soul, greatly increasing the group's power to serve, not through control or individual will but individual will subordinated to the will of the soul which is conscious of its relationship to a greater whole.

As with the disciples of Christ, two thousand years ago, the serving members of a group experience a greater sense of accomplishment from contact with the energy that flows from the higher Buddhic levels. In the new earth, when the spiritual Hierarchy or Fifth Kingdom is in process of externalizing, such flow of energy will become more common.

This law assists individuals and groups in developing a sensitivity to and impression from the soul and the Fifth Kingdom, just as the Law of Vibration works to develop the personalities sensitivity to its environment.

In the new era, when this law will help bring about magnificent edifices for the purpose of spiritual instruction, group work and initiation. Humanity and the Fifth Kingdom will cooperate in their manifestation. They will be Temples of Good, displaying the greatest beauty humanity has ever seen, and they will be egalitarian for all to experience.

These divine edifices will honor God and the Path of Return for humanity. One of these divine edifices will be in the southwestern quadrant of the United States. It has already been designed and exists in the etheric realm of the earth. It is called The Templar[40] by its master architects—spiritual Elders of the Fifth Kingdom.

"This is the Temple of the most difficult initiatory processes. The reason for this difficulty and for the importance of this Temple is due to the fact that our solar system is a system of Love. We shall then have a new world—one which will express the light, the love and the knowledge of God."[41] This statement by the Teacher DK sums up the essential message of this law: It is the Christ Impulse which drives the soul onward in its return home and in the process world's are redeemed.

15. LAW OF ENLIGHTENMENT OR CONTINUITY OF CONSCIOUSNESS

This is the great healing Law of separative consciousness. It deals with the continuity between the superconscious and the consciousness which develops upon the path of self-transformation, which in turn, opens the doors to enlightenment.

Continuity of consciousness dispels separation and enables one to consciously participate with the Fifth Kingdom, and the initiate to utilize time as a factor in the great plan of evolution, and receive impressions from the Mind of God.

The physical universe is a living energy system in a continuous and endless process of renewal and creation where everything in life is interconnected with the consciousness evolving within it.

The same can be said about the personality. Both are physical entities with an indwelling consciousness. It may be surprising to learn that a human being, a planetary logos, a solar logos a universal logos, etc. are all developing continuity of consciousness, unique to their level of mastery which means that enlightenment is also progressive.

A very high enlightenment is an unshatterable state of no separation and a living continuity of relationship in one's consciousness. The Teacher DK calls this state of enlightenment "isolated unity"[42], one of the most puzzling concepts for the unenlightened mind to comprehend. It is a state of "unfettered enlightenment" enabling the initiate to participate with great freedom in the life of our planetary Logos. It enabled the Buddha and the Christ to point to the goal and indicate the Way, showing how humanity could also tread the Lighted Way.

One of the goals of education in the new era that the planned work of the Christ will be involved with, will be the continuity of consciousness. The Avatars of love and wisdom have always brought to humanity the revelation of hope and the incentive for a fuller spiritual life.

It is the transformation of knowledge into wisdom and of mind into an enlightened

---

[40] The story of the Templar was first published in a book called: The Templar, A Divine Edifice for the coming golden age.

[41] Esoteric Psychology II, p. 280 .

[42] that stage of consciousness which sees the whole as one and knows itself, as fact, as identified with that whole. It is a whole which is "isolated" in the consciousness of the man, and not the man himself who regards himself as isolated. The word "unity" expresses his relationship to the whole.

mind that enables the individual to establish the continuity of consciousness within his or her awareness. When there is continuity of consciousness, the brain of the newborn through the enlightened mind, retains the experience of the soul, between reincarnations and at the moment of rebirth.

This law governs the science of the Antahkarana which is under the greater science of Light. The science of the Antahkarana has two phases. For the spiritual aspirant, it bridges the personality and the soul and later for the advanced disciple, it bridges the soul-infused personality and spirit. It is the second phase that produces liberation from rebirth and full continuity of consciousness.

The Law of Service plays an integral role in the continuity of consciousness. The goal is not the liberation of the soul, but the redemption of matter, through an enlightened consciousness that takes matter and builds forms into more perfect expressions of life. It is why this law is associated with the term "occult saving".

"The spiritual path may feel solitary but it is not a path of loneliness"[43], says the Teacher DK. Continuity of consciousness is a living continuity of sensed relationship expressed in the words: "I am one with the light that shines through my soul, my brothers and my Master."

The key to continuity of consciousness is identification with the soul. Therefore, it is necessary to practice staying identified while continuing the self-purification as needed. The problem is that the individual intends to remain identified with the soul, but ever so often forgets. The lower mind has the weakness of forgetting. This requires the strengthening of the will to maintain the tension necessary for the development of the continuity of consciousness.

Even knowledge that is received from books is easily forgotten. Therefore, the knowledge of the continuity of consciousness cannot be acquired through books, but through persistent practice of soul identification. This builds a purified etheric body—the golden body of light. The Taoists call it "the golden satchel" and the Platonist calls it "Augoeides" (the luminous body).

Once the energy of the purified etheric body is stabilized, the consciousness of the initiated human being can continue from incarnation to incarnation without loss of memory or knowledge. One of the purposes of initiation is the stabilization of energy.

Prior to stabilization, after leaving the body, the consciousness loses the memory of the knowledge that has been accumulated by the soul at the time of rebirth, and much of the knowledge gained in the previous life is lost. Thus, slow and cumbersome progress from life to life is made. Even if the knowledge of the previous incarnation is not immediately recalled, it can easily be triggered by a book, something someone says, or by reflection.

As human beings continue to ascend in consciousness, they acquire higher bodies of light. The highest of these, to the ancient Egyptians is called the "merkaba" (body of pure light), which allows for inter-dimensional travel, just as a car is used for transportation, communication with higher beings of light, and transmission of information.

---

[43] Discipleship in the New Age, Vol. II, p. 647

As humanity advances along the Path of Light, the opportunity opens up to be of greater service, The new Sciences that work the subtler energies of color and sound will accelerate the enlightenment process. This will be greatly facilitated, as mentioned by the manifestation of divine edifices such as The Templar.

A first step toward enlightenment begins when the effort is taken to simply be aware non-judgmentally of thoughts, emotions and actions, to simply be the inner observer. The practice of being the observer purifies the etheric body which raises the vibration of the atoms and transmutes the grey matter of the brain.

Guatama and Jesus after many lifetimes, removed the final veils of ignorance and made contact the divine Light of truth and love. Jesus and Guatama then understood the meaning of the word "emptiness"- the emptiness of ego. That which appears to be separate is nothing but an illusion and those who follow the path of separateness, must remain on the wheel of rebirth. By following the examples of the great ones, the individual sets in motion the movement towards enlightened being.

Enlightenment is not easy to see in others. Buddha simply described it as "I am awake". When one is awake like that of the Buddha or Christ, one is a force for enlightenment in the world.

There is a distinction between the coming event many are anticipating that is being called the "Shift" and what this law describes as the continuity of consciousness. The shift involves a transition from a physical state to an etheric state. It will not stabilize or expand consciousness in that sense.

The Shift will enable the earth and those who have prepared themselves to continue their evolution from where they left off, on a higher more refined etheric level of existence, in less dense and lighter substance.

The consequent change in form is what is unprecedented about the Shift. At death, a physical conversion does not happen and there is only the release of the soul from its shell and the plane of matter. The Shift will allow the soul to remain with the form as the body goes through a transformation in vibratory frequency. Perhaps Jesus was referring to the Shift when he said: "New wine cannot be put into old wineskins".

The shift will be experienced at different levels of consciousness, from fully conscious, to a deep meditative-like state, to semi-conscious, to unconscious. But, regardless, all the souls who cross the threshold will find themselves in new more light-filled bodies.

For those who are less prepared, the apparent disorientation will naturally subside. For those who have developed continuity of consciousness it will be neither traumatic nor unfamiliar, but a continuation of the kind of subtle experiences already known to intuitive souls.

During the shift, all will experience an acceleration and a transformation. It is nothing to fear. Simply relax and enjoy the ride. Those who remain identified with physical form will feel from its loss. Learning in each present moment to let go of attachments to form is good preparation. Also, each expression of love, the light causes the atoms and cells of the body to become brighter and vibrates at a higher rate. This will make entry into the new earth a very harmonious and enjoyable experience.

When the shift happens, for those human souls who can maintain their inner equilibrium despite the outer chaos, will find the transition as one continuous conscious experience.

As identification with the soul steadily progresses, so will humanity's enlightenment. The following is a verse from one of the Masters on enlightenment:

"Simple are the Master's words, you say? To the intellectual, it may be only mental stimulation and entertainment.
The more intelligent, the less one believes.
Better is the student who is simple-minded, for the heart is easier to reach.
Stronger is the spirit who accepts the Master's word.
There have been many more people who have reached the doorsteps of enlightenment, than those who have professed genius."[44]

16. LAW OF HIERARCHY OR CO-CREATION

This law is privy to a great reservoir of power and those highest manifestations of divine love, truth and beauty. It is the Law that guides all beings of light that work with the three of the most highly evolved Orders of the universe.

Within the great chain of Being, there are many Orders that are spiritualized and liberated, each a force of enlightenment and redemption. "Forces of Light" is a general term used to describe any or all of the universal brotherhoods of eternal love and light, be they of human or devic (angelic) origin, or a fusion of both.

There is a ladder of consciousness in the universe, the rungs of which represent

progressive expansions of consciousness. The higher the rung, the greater the consciousness and greater the responsibility for evolutionary progress. This is co-measurement.

What is Hierarchy? Firstly, a redefinition and reformulation of the word hierarchy is needed. Earthly organizational structures are overly layered and autocratically administered because they do not operate out of unity, inner spiritual authority or alignment with divine law. Human hierarchies are largely governed by selfishness and greed. As evolution continues, the spiritual values of this law will replace those of today's economic, political and educational systems.

Secondly, imagine a ladder. Each ascending rung representing an attainable stage in the evolution of consciousness. At the top of the ladder is a blazing light of boundless Intelligence, Power and Love that directs the life of the Whole universe.

Every rung is governed by specific laws and has its hierarchies of light, marked by greater levels of responsibility.

The spiritual hierarchy of Earth is governed by the cosmic ray of divine wisdom and love. Its members (of the 5th kingdom) are graduated humans who have attained mastery over the human condition and have accepted the responsibility for guiding humanity and formulating the Plan based on Logoic purpose.

As more of humanity's soul unfolds and the Fifth Kingdom externalizes, humanity and the lower kingdoms benefit. This again is co-measurement. This leads to goal-fitness where humanity becomes the intermediary between the three lower evolutions: the mineral, the vegetable and the animal

---

[44] 1994 -1997, Letter

kingdoms and the three higher spiritual evolutions: the soul, the planetary lives, and the solar lives. For the lower lives also require the unfoldment of consciousness.

The Fifth Kingdom is never static. Just as human beings evolve into ever-expanding levels of consciousness, so to do members of the Fifth Kingdom, moving on to greater spheres of life and service.

At the same time, the Fifth Kingdom has need of incarnate souls to implement aspects of the Plan on the outer planes. When potential co-workers are identified, they are helped along in myriad ways. The universe is constantly evolving with divine directives issuing from solar and cosmic levels.

There are three main Orders in this, our universe, which is directed by Hierarchies of Light:

1. The Order of Michael: Coordinates the Hierarchies of Protection; protects the galaxies from the interference of the lower or dark forces, except where necessary to test/train for soul progression.

2. The Order of Melchizedek: Coordinates the teaching, education and consciousness programs. The Office of the Christ is in this order. The Spiritual Hierarchy is under the Office of the Christ. These orders are bridges, connective links that establish the relationship between the outer and the inner or physical - spiritual creation on order to advance evolution.

3. The Order of Enoch: responsible for divine revelation, spiritual science and higher knowledge for the initiation the faithful into new worlds of consciousness. This Order builds the pyramidal grids on planets to evolve biomes of intelligence. Responsible for the building of higher evolutionary architecture—temples of light and initiation. Responsible for all spiritual-scientific scrolls of Knowledge. The builders of living bio-computers and living bio-satellites. Responsible for transmitting the scientific keys of Living Light into worlds.

4. The three above Orders coordinate their programs and cooperate on a vast scale beyond human comprehension. Their level of enlightenment and attainment of higher bodies enables them to do so.

Co-creation is a continuous manifestation of Divine Purpose through the cooperation of countless beings of light who receive directives from Divine Source. This sums up the concept of Hierarchy. The message of this law is: as humanity ascends the ladder of life it must also bring the lower kingdoms of nature up with it. Jesus affirmed the law when he said: "I can of mine own self do nothing."

The lack of enlightened awareness has kept humanity imprisoned in the lower hierarchies of power and social systems. A spiritual Hierarchy consists of beings of enlightened wisdom, working together as a unified organism fulfilling divine purpose.

The One Reality with its evolution in consciousness through an infinite variety of forms is made possible, because of this great law. When this is understood, humanity, will realize that cooperation and service is the crown of Self-hood. The redemption of worlds relies this law. Hierarchy itself is the foundation and expression of universal justice, working fairly and justly with all the Laws.

The primary role of the earth's spiritual Hierarchy is the elevation of human consciousness for the fulfillment of Logoic purpose and will.

The great Chain of Hierarchy is responsible for moving creation along its path of evolutionary unfoldment. In our little solar system, the responsibility of our Solar Logos for the solar system is:

1. Development of consciousness leading to Recognition
2. Refinement of form through the expression of Love-Wisdom
3. Intensification of realized life leading to the fulfillment of the Law of Love.

This is a direct result of our Solar Logos reaching a level of consciousness where the purity of love must manifest before the next and highest aspect of divinity, divine will and power can be utilized for evolutionary purposes.

Hierarchy in its most general of terms is simply a description of enlightened collaborative work. Each co-worker in an enlightened hierarchy works to further the evolution of consciousness and to fulfill the will of the Nameless One. This law deals with the process of ascension. Ascension is only possible through collaborative service and conscious cooperation—there is no other measure for ascension!

In the ways of this law, none can bring about advancement of the soul, unless the united work is for others. "From the spiritual Hierarchy's side, Co-creation involves a narrowing of the flow of descending energy into a funnel that feeds into the upward-ascending channel built by disciples. Disciples on the path evoke knowledge from the spiritual Hierarchy and They respond by transmitting, through etheric substance, ideas that are useful to disseminate in a given period. There is a distorted idea that human beings can act as divine co-creators with one another. Among human beings, cooperation

is possible. Only when human beings work in conscious cooperation with the Kingdom of Souls is Co-creation or Co-authorship possible. Its purpose is to bring ideas and impulses of divine origin into the awareness of the human race."[45].

There are the "fallen" that seek to thwart God's will and plan, but there is the One Power and the One Law that they cannot thwart, God. The three great orders as mentioned above, have the responsibility of dealing with cosmic evil or the "fallen ones."

The great Chain of Hierarchy is responsible for moving evolution along and the redemption of worlds which the "fallen" have corrupted. Humanity is responsible for the redemption of its own evil as a result of human caused karma, and the sense of this is entering human consciousness.

Human evolution began when God's image and likeness, the individualized spirit soul was placed as a seed form of His will into His pattern of creation. This is the law that governs the directing of evolutionary advancement throughout all of God's creation.

"I of my own small self
can do nothing,
But I, the True Self,
am co-creating a New World
in the company of kindred souls."[46]

17. LAW OF POLARITY

This law works closely with the laws of electricity and is important in the study of force or energy in man and in groups, and in

---

[45] atreeoflight.org: Cosmic Whisperings - New Human Beings

[46] 11 February, 2024, Letter

the subjective interpretation of the human family in terms of electrical phenomena, positive and negative charges. A case in point is "original sin" (a religious interpretation) which is merely the scission of unity into duality and is only considered a "sin" when judged objectively.

To the eye of the soul, opposites are simply complementary aspects whose merging produces unity, just as in the physics of light certain superimposed colors, result in a colorless white light. For the human brain, polarity is necessary in order for the human being to perceive the objective world of nature.

This law is beyond rational analysis, but not so for the soul, which is closer to the one single unique source of energy that binds all things. Everything in manifestation is dual and has poles, remembering that everything created issued from the one cosmic source of energy. The purpose of this law, in relation to human evolution, is to show what the obstacles are to the personality as it treads the path of ascent.

"The polarity of a man, of a group and of a congery of groups, the polarity of planets and their relationship to each other and to the Sun, the polarity of the solar system and its relationship to other systems, the polarity of one plane to another, and of one principle to another, the polarity of subtler vehicles, and the scientific application of the laws of electricity to the totality of existence on the physical plane will bring about a revolution upon the planet second only to that effected at the time of individualization."[47]

Polarity is behind the universal sex impulse. To create, the Absolute All transformed a fragment of itself into spirit and matter. Everything has a positive or negative polarity. Without the Law of Polarity, light, gravity and electricity would not be possible. On the mental plane, this principle manifests itself in the psyche of each person in degrees of enlightened or shadowed mind.

Without duality, there could be no discernment or conscience. Discernment is the power of the mind to negate that which is of the not-self, which allows the soul to overcome the bondage of the personality. Liberation or freedom from the three worlds and rebirth begins with the power to recognize and negate the not-self. This law is at the heart of walking the middle path of neutrality, not in passivity, but consciously and actively between the opposites.

The diversity of nature is the result of the devic kingdom working with this and other laws. Evolution results from life's passage through the complementary opposites of the unbalanced poles to perfect equilibrium, through which the greater universe passes. Nothing in manifestation that is perceptible, is so by itself. Polarity is required for manifestation and perception.

Everything in the universe has its opposite, its complement. As long as thinking is duality based, truth is relative. With human physical awareness, opposites can be known, but not both at the same time. It is only in the realms expanded consciousness that the objective world of matter and the subjective world spirit can be reconciled into unity. Only expanded consciousness can see beyond duality and this is brought about by treading the path of spiritual transformation - becoming the soul

---

in form. In the transformation of consciousness there is no loss of individuality. In fact, individuality is actually expanded, fuller and more whole, because it has been spiritualized.

Many of the humanity's problems are due to unbalanced polarity thinking, causing such thinking to be revealed. Only balanced polarity thinking and balanced interchange can balance unbalanced polarity. This requires a transformation of consciousness. If this law had been rightly understood, earth would have already be on a higher turn of the evolutionary spiral. Both, the Buddha with his teaching of the noble eight-fold path (or the middle way) and the Christ with his teachings on self-transformation and love, came to show the balanced way.

The complete maxim of the Pythagoras' school was: "Know Thyself," "Know the Self," "Know the One", pointing out that the path was progressive. It lead from knowledge of the soul, to knowledge of the monad, to and knowledge of the One Life, through the transformation and expansion of consciousness, enabling one to know the universe as it is, a phenomenon of polarity pervaded by an unchanging absolute unity.

In the book, The Study of Number by R.A. Schwaller de Lubicz, a student of the Mystery School teachings, says: "The irreducible One possesses a double nature, and this double nature, which is passive and active respectively, must manifest itself. The Irreducible One is equally Feminine and Masculine in its absolute nature and exists as such in potentiality only, but its manifest nature is not androgynous. The One is recognized by its double nature to be Two. The Uncaused, Causal One manifests and becomes the Two, a new unity which is reducible. Such is the manifested nature of the Irreducible One." This statement that the reducible reveals the irreducible is worth pondering.

Each mind must resolve this "sphinx" of the One and the Two, for itself. This is the great mystery. It is the human brain that separates the elements of these extreme positions into opposing parts, causing cycles of conflict.

However, it is the Law of Polarity that makes possible the choices we make on the scale of life between good and evil, right and wrong, generosity and greed, love and fear, truth and lies. This law establishes the dual aspect of reality. Everything that is, has its double. Positive and negative, light and darkness, hot and cold, love and fear, mortality and immortality, light and darkness, right and left—these are all siblings of one another.

Polarities are in essence, inseparable from one another, for the meaning of their terms is relative. Therefore, good is not good and bad is not bad, except in relation to one another, when perceived as such by the human brain. Nothing of itself is positive and nothing of itself is negative. Opposites only appear as such to unenlightened human consciousness. Like every Master and Initiate that has graduated from the earth density of duality, the Law of Polarity must be faced while in incarnation and its nature transcended. Blessed are those who know the truth, for "the truth will set you free".

"Thou who read life
mostly read it as black and white.
The imprint of mind says it to be so.

Blessed is the one who does not submit
to the Law of Duality,
but honors all Laws of the Universe.

*There are many shades of grey between light
and dark.
But blessed is the one who finds
the middle road of neutrality."*

-Master KH
(17 October 1995, Letter)

18. *LAWS OF ELECTRICITY*

This law is plural because of the truth that there is nothing in manifestation but electricity with its many manifestations and perpetual transmutations, as stated in The Secret Doctrine by H.P. Blavatsky. As just mentioned in the previous law, everything in the cosmos is dual in nature. But, this law goes one step further, by stating that, that which is dual expresses itself in manifestation as three qualities: positive - negative - neutral.

Life itself is electricity, but all that material science knows today is that which is only the physical aspect of electricity.

In the new era, as humanity moves into a relationship with the soul and a greater understanding of its own threefold nature, these laws will be increasingly studied and applied.

This law deals with the three manifestations of electricity or cosmic fire. Electricity as used in this law is a word synonymous with the words "life" or "fire" (fire, being the highest of the four elements:

1. Fire by Friction: manifests as the physical or objective realm; form; the lowest manifestation of electricity. Descriptive of earth's material culture.

2. Solar Fire: manifests as the soul or subjective realm of consciousness; Our solar system is concerned with this fire and it blending with fire by friction. All potentiality lis in the enlivening of Solar Fire. The intermediate manifestation of electricity. Descriptive of Venusian spiritual culture.

3. Electric Fire: manifests as the realm of pure spirit; energy, life; the highest manifestation of electricity; a substance so radiant and alive that it is impossible to define or describe. Descriptive of Sirius' culture of synthesis.

As mentioned earlier in the Law of Polarity, the one primordial energy becomes and vitalizes the many types of consciousness and form. Electricity also manifests itself according to the seven levels of existence that make up the totality of our solar system. In an ascending scale, electricity is: objective form on the physical levels, emotion on the astral levels, thought-enlightened thought on the lower-higher mental levels, intuition on the buddhic levels, divine will-purpose on atmic levels, isolated unity on the monadic plane and divine creative spirit on logoic levels.

In a human being we have:

1. Electricity as it manifests through the personality, called "*fire by friction*"—the intelligent activity of matter. This form of electricity makes possible the soul to acquire experience in the three worlds of human evolution.

2. Electricity as it manifests through the soul, called "*solar fire*"—the activity of consciousness. This electricity makes possible the unfolding of the soul.

3. Electricity as it manifests through the monad, called *"electric fire"* — the activity of Spirit. This electricity brings manifestation to its highest form of development

It was the Teacher DK in his Treatise On Cosmic Fire by Alice A. Bailey, His amanuensis, that the nature of electricity was introduced, nearly 100 years ago.

Electricity is the one primordial energy that never leaves its unchanging state of synthesis, yet manifests as three vibratory qualities for the purpose of evolution. This is part of the mystery of electricity. All of evolution is vitalized by and permeated with cosmic fire.

The internal combustion engine, the burning of fossil fuels and nuclear fission are products of fire by friction consciousness. As soul consciousness evolves, fire by friction will be replaced by solar fire consciousness, forms of energy.

The Teacher DK, in the books by Alice A. Bailey, has said, referring to the new era, that as humanity's consciousness evolves the true Mysteries will be restored and revealed. He says they "will reveal themselves through science and the incentive to search for them there will be given by the Christ. The Mysteries contain, within their formulas and teachings, the key to the science which will unlock the mystery of electricity—the greatest spiritual science and area of divine knowledge in the world, the fringes of which have only just been touched." There is much in His words worth pondering.

The laws of electricity as they relate to the expansion of consciousness will find their application with scientific precision in the coming temples of Initiation. In Alice A. Bailey's, "A Treatise Cosmic Fire" it states: "Every initiate, presented to the Initiator, is accompanied by two of the Masters, who stand one on either side of him. The three of them together form a triangle which makes the work possible. Two points of the triangle represent each a different polarity, and one point represents the point of equilibrium, of synthesis or merging."

In the work of Initiation, in the applying of electric and solar solar fire to consciousness, triangulation is important. The triangle is the strongest and most stable of shapes, enabling the balanced flow of energy.

Initiation is a process by which the initiate uses available energies to bring about an intensification, expansion and stabilization of energy within one's bodies. Through imparted knowledge, initiation allows cosmic fire energy to be controlled and manipulated by the initiate for evolutionary purposes.

As mentioned, all energy is electrical in nature and there is nothing but electricity in manifestation. In each initiation, the initiate experiences an expansion and stabilization of energy. It is in these initiations that the initiate begins to have a realization of the true meaning of electricity.

Fire by friction animates the atoms of matter, or the substance of the dense physical solar system, and results in the spheroidal form of an atom and a planet. It provides the innate heat of all spheres and is responsible for the differentiation of atoms, one from another, as attested by the periodic table of elements.

Solar fire animates forms or conglomerations of atoms, resulting in coherent group formations; the spiritual radiation of light and love and their magnetic interaction. As mentioned, solar fire is what our solar Logos is seeking to express through the solar system.

This law, that is coming in to the fore will help humanity understand how electricity works and can be used, under the direction of the Christ, for fulfilling the purpose of our planetary Logos.

Tapping into the cosmic fire of the universe requires an understanding of the laws of electricity. George Van Tassel, in his book, *When Stars Look Down*, said: "God is the infinity of an infinite electric universe that thought atoms, solar systems and galaxies into being."

The study of this law will give humanity the understanding and an intimate experience of the intricate web of life. Humanity's just apprehension of this law and its mysteries will come about, as he studies himself, and knows himself to be a unity of triple fire, manifesting in many aspects.

19. *LAW OF CYCLES, ALTERATION OR PERIODICITY*

This is a Law of great interest. All things happen according to the Law of Cycles, Alteration or Periodicity. Consciousness evolves by alternation, accomplished by regeneration and renewal. Alternation, the swing of the pendulum is the mechanical image of livingness or life in action, in progression.

The propagation of waves is a symbol of the alternating nature of life, in the simple way a hand causes a rope to curl or in the way wind or gravitational pull causes the waves of water. There is the time-space element to a wave and the energy element in its amplitude, thus waves measure time, space and energy. Correspondingly, this law expresses the Trinity of God: Time, Space and Being.

Each aspect of life in manifestation has its cyclic poles of opposition: Time, with its "Then" and "Now". Space, with its "Here" and "There" and Being, with its "Involution" and "Evolution". All evolution submits to this great law.

This law, which shows Being manifesting through action, is in itself proof that you have always been and always will be. Being's poles can also be seen as "life" and death". Not death in the conventional sense, but the ability of substance to change, to conform to the requirements of a new environment. This statement holds a clue to understanding the Shift event that is on the horizon.

The day expresses and recedes and expresses again, recedes again. Likewise, the night. Likewise full moon, the new moon. Everything is an alternating function. Universal Mind created all forms of life everywhere and manifests the continuous activity of life. The interesting thing about cycles is that they all reach a peak, end and begin again, never repeating themselves exactly.

Earth is in an unprecedented cycle of transformation that depends on choice. Each person must now choose between two worlds, a world of love and unity or a world of selfish materialism, inequality and lawlessness. The key to entering into the new era, as mentioned earlier, is a consciousness of specific vibrational frequency.

Unless Spirit is acknowledged and higher guidance used for self-transformation, the injustices and cruelties of human life set in motion relentless cycles of conflict for those who remain entangled in them. Cycles will simply repeat themselves until it is learned that only when consciousness changes, will the world change. This law is a great teacher of choice.

The cycles of major extinctions of life forms on earth are not random but an intricate part of the interconnected web of evolution. Every detail in the life cycles of an age, a human being and a planet is recorded by a vast web of electrical filaments called Akasha. Souls cycle through lifetimes of incarnations. Solar ages and seasons cycle through the movement of the earth around the sun. Great Solar Ages cycle through the movement of the sun around the galactic center. Cycles control lifespans of great beings in manifestation.

All previous planetary cycles have prepared the ground for the cycle of a divine purpose that awaits Earth and humanity. The cyclical wheels of destiny have been moving toward this time for millions of years, to make humanity aware that there is a Plan. To fulfill the plan, humanity must become an active participant in the Plan.

In ages past and present, the divine purpose for Earth's evolution has been transmitted by the Planetary Logos to the spiritual Hierarchy for formulation into the plan. It is now time that humanity take responsibility for its part in the implementation of the plan.

Why all our effort to understand this law? It has a profound message related to the Law of Service. Alice A. Bailey in her book, From Intellect to Intuition says: "The search in the world goes on; the cry of humanity rises from the depths and mounts to the very throne of God Himself. From the heart of the Temple of God, to which we may have fought and wrestled our way, we turn back and work on earth. We rest not in our endeavor till the last of the world's seekers has found his way home."

Humankind is destined to work intelligently with the Law of Alternation.

Periods of outer activity follow periods of inner rest and periods of recognition alternate with periods of apparent silence. If the student on the path evolves as desired, each period of rest is followed by one of greater activity, and of more potent achievement. Rhythm, ebb and flow, and the measured beat of the pulsating life are always the great Law of the universe. In learning to respond to the vibration of the high places, this law must be borne in mind.

This quote from the Tao Te Ching of Lao Tzu: "Nature does not hurry, yet everything is accomplished." sums up the wisdom this law holds. In times of rest, in tune with the ebb and flow of life, we can pause and reflect and can gain new perspectives. There are times when a reassessment is needed between the rhythm of individual purpose and that of the larger picture. This is why the quality of group rhythm will becomes important in the new era.

The life of soul unfoldment need not be a frantic pursuit. It can and should be a life of service through action that embraces the flow of life, trusting in the wisdom of this law.

This great law governs all manifestation, whether it be the manifestation of a solar Logos through the medium of a solar system, or the manifestation of a soul through the medium of a body. The Law of Alternation continually introduces the new and terminates the old, and likewise governs all the kingdoms of nature.

Attuning to the ebbs and flow of life supports the life of the soul and the group. The Law of Love is connected with this law because it controls the equality of rhythm. Can unevenness of rhythm exist in the soul, whose nature is love?

If one wants to discover the secret of peace, it is important to understand that everything in the universe works through attraction, repulsion, continuously, with the least possible effort, with the proper adjustment of balance, and with the necessary rhythm. This is an extremely important law and working with it is crucial if humanity is to establish genuine peace.

20. LAW OF UNIVERSAL HARMONICS

This law like the laws of electricity is plural because it functions differently depending on the level of manifestation on which it operates. It governs the harmonic unity of forms or parts in relation to one another and the whole.

It is a law which operates through and is natural to the devic kingdom. It governs the archetypal patterns of perfect Mind. It is the living mathematics of divine mind. It relates proportional form to harmonic unity. The soul is a harmonic unit of energy in the form of light and consciousness. Harmonic unity can take many natural forms and uses the mathematics of proportion to do so.

Its divine mathematics allows for infinite creativity and freedom. It is a Law of harmonic proportion that allows form and energy to function harmoniously. It will enable the human kingdom and devic intelligences to work together creatively. From the application of this law arises all just and balanced good works.

Many of this law's secrets have been valued and guarded by the ancient Mystery Schools, the Masonic Order, the Mevlevi Order and others. One of the most revered of sacred symbols, the Tetrad of Pythagoras, which consist of ten points arranged in four rows: one, two, three, and four points in each row. It is a geometrical symbol, that to the Pythagoreans, represented the "music (or harmony) of the spheres", a term used by philosophers and astronomers that is synonymous with universal harmonics.

The first four numbers of the Tetrad or as it is commonly called the Tetraktys, represent:

1. Monad – Unity, Oneness
2. Dyad – Twoness, Otherness
3. Triad – Harmony, Balance
4. Tetrad – Kosmos, Manifestation

The four rows add up to ten, which is unity of a higher order. The importance of this law from which the Tetrad's sacred symbolism flows cannot overstated. This law, which the Tetrad represents in its seed-like form, covers the principles of the natural world, the harmony of the cosmos, the ascent to the divine, and the mysteries of the divine realm.

The ancient philosopher-scientists addressed a prayer to the sacred symbol:

"Bless us, divine number, thou who generated gods and men! O holy, holy Tetraktys, thou that containest the root and source of the eternally flowing creation! For the divine number begins with the profound, pure unity until it comes to the holy four; then it begets the mother of all, the all-comprising, all-bounding, the first-born, the never-swerving, the never-tiring holy ten, the keyholder of all"

In the book Letters on Occult Meditation by Alice A. Bailey, the Teacher DK devotes several pages, using the analogy of musical intervals and ratios, to show how the basic note or major third of the personality (5:4), the dominant fifth of the soul (3:2) and the ultimate seventh or full chord or octave of the monad (2:1) relate to the spiritual path of ascent. All these musical ratios can be found in the Tetrad.

This law through the principle of harmonic unity brings about an equality of one ratio to another through the principle of proportion. Right proportion is at the heart of this law which supports all life and growth.

It is the proportion of gases in our planet's atmosphere and the proportion of atmospheric pressure to volume within the earths atmosphere and lungs that allows physical act of breathing to take place. Many artists, scientists and philosophers are familiar with what is called the divine proportion responsible for giving us in nature the spiral of the nautilus and galaxies.

When the cosmic ray of harmony once again becomes active in 2025, this law will take on more prominence. It is this law which informs the cosmic ray of harmony.

The new age is bringing this law into manifestation and with it, knowledge of some of its operations used by highly evolved, perfected beings for the harmonic attunement of consciousness on planets that are evolving from materiality into spirituality.

Axiatonal lines (a term used in the book The Keys of Enoch) are lines of highly refined etheric substance, which exist throughout the macrocosm, connecting planets, suns, and galaxies with one another. They form a vast matrix of pathways for energy to flow. These axiatonal lines are similar to the meridians of traditional Chinese medicine that carry life energy, prana or chi to all parts of the human microcosm or physical-etheric body of man.

The great directing forces of evolution in our universe, use axiatonal lines to transmit along them specific codes of light and sound for the purpose of raising a planet's vibration and its life forms to higher levels of consciousness, perfection and wholeness.

Axiatonal lines also have their correspondence in the earth's meridian system of ley lines, grid lines and vortexes. At these vortexes can be found many of the world's greatest examples of architecture, such as pyramids, cathedrals, temples and sacred sites. These vortexia, harmonically and geometrically distributed around the planet, connect the life energy of our planetary Logos to that of the earth's.

When the science of the "antahkarana"[48] is better understood and used to bring about the merging of the soul and the personality, the function of axiatonal lines in relation to the evolution of consciousness, knowledge of the five higher bodies of light (mentioned earlier): 1. the eka body, 2. the electro-magnetic body, 3. the epi-kenetic body, 4. the gematria body and 5. the merkaba body or divine light vehicle,[49] and their use will be taught.

"You have asked what the new Science of Light will be in the fifth dimension. All geometric shapes, such as those that are found, for example, in sacred vortices around and within the earth will be fourth and fifth dimensional, similar in appearance to the platonic solids and hybrid platonic solids you know of today. Various light-geometry-resonance sciences such as holography, sacred geometry, crystal formation, sound

---

48 the consciousness bridge built using meditation, between the personality and the soul.

49To know more about the five higher bodes of light, see The Keys of Enoch, by J.J. Hurtak, and the Nag Hammadi

harmonics, color and vibrational healing, symbols, soul fusion and in a more complicated setting vortex-based mathematics, to name a few, will all fall under this future science. The Science of Light will be the backbone of all study encompassing matter, force, energy, light as substance and its relationship to nature, the cosmos and the evolving consciousness of man. At the heart of this Science of Light lie the Law of Balance, the golden divine ratio, the decimal numbers of pi, and symmetry all having to do with cosmic consciousness, fractals, geometry, abstract mentalism and the higher dimensions."[50]"

This law, working in conjunction with the Science of Light will transform human culture and the planet in ways never before possible. As the higher laws and spiritual sciences are better understood, a balance between consciousness and form will manifest as harmony in every aspect of life. "At the heart of this Science of Light lies the Law of Balance, the golden divine ratio of phi, the decimal numbers of pi, and dynamic symmetry all having to do with cosmic consciousness, fractals, geometry, abstract mentalism and the higher dimensions. The divine universe was created by energy as a means to expand itself into matter. In metaphysical theory that was the very first act of balance...balancing spiritual energy to physical matter. So in essence one could say that balance is the key that unlocks the secrets of the universe."[51]

The pentagram's divine proportions symbolize perfected humanity. It is used by the Fifth Kingdom at the time of the full moon, when the sun is in Taurus, to set up a particular harmonic which attracts or invokes the Buddha for his blessing once a year. Alice A. Bailey in The Rays and Initiations gives an account of this: "Hence we have the activity of the Buddha at the May Full Moon and that of the Christ at the following June Full Moon. Their united activity serves to bring about a much closer approach between the Lord of the World and the Hierarchy, via His four highly evolved "Great Lords": the Buddha, the Christ, the Manu, and the Mahachohan—the five points of energy which are creating the five-pointed star of Humanity at this time."

The six pointed star is representative of the devic kingdom. The union of the five pointed star and six pointed star is a construction in geometry that represents symbolically the union of complementary opposites such as the microcosm and macrocosm. The union of the hexagon and pentagon is a represents unity and interrelationship, Someday, it will manifest as the union between, and cooperation of, the human and devic kingdoms.

The great mystery and knowledge of the God proportion: phi, found in the five pointed star, is divinely connected to creation itself, in the scission of unity. The beauty that will abound from the understanding and application of this law, with its geometry and divine mathematics will be nurtured by the cosmic ray of harmony. The spirit of love combined with divine knowledge, in the new era, will motivate humanity, to discover the truth about form and the life which brought it into the light of day.

Once the truth, that form conceals is discovered, form will neither veil nor hide

---

[50] 29 July 2013, Letter

[51] ibid

the truth, but will seen as a means of revealing all the radiance of God (Her+His power and magnetism), revealing all there is of form, of life, of beauty and usefulness.

This law guides the laws of form, it provides the knowledge Beauty which preserves Unity and gives us a glimpse into the Mind of God, as the Divine Geometer.

21. *LAW OF UNIVERSALITY*

The universe is the sum total of all things visible and invisible that fill infinite space. It is the great whole composed of all its parts. The universe is the boundless immutable principle in expression.

The human heart beats in a determined periodicity with its systole and diastole, numerically, in accord with the heart of the universe. This is the pulse of love that pulsates through the universe in divine rhythm.

When the great sages speak of man (man as humankind, not gender) as the microcosm, they are speaking of man as a manifestation stage of the macrocosm. They are saying that man is a seed-form of the universe. This is the mystery that has baffled many a philosopher and spiritual seeker.

The word "man" has its root in the Sanskrit word "Manas", which means "mind" and as mentioned, not man as gender. Manas reflects the evolutionary advance of consciousness. Man is the image and similitude of God. Man is created out of God substance and similar. This is the truth that this law holds and upholds. When this is realized in consciousness, when there is a spiritual re-identification with the whole, man solves the mystery of the Sphinx, the

great mystery of the Pyramid and the mystery of the Self.

As long as a person perceives with limited mind, there will be necessarily be a separation between the partial and the universal. On the other hand, when one realizes the great mystery, all boundaries and separations disappear. A mystery remains a mystery until the truth it veils, is realized in consciousness.

The universe is bound together in a single system and operates as a single unit. But, how did the universe come into being? It came into being by thought or perfect mind and into manifestation by vibration, "In the beginning was the word".

Man uses the same principle of manas or mind for creative expression, but man doesn't think of himself as being in every part of the universe and the universe in him. Nor does man think that it is the mental vitality of his thoughts which have brought all his creations into form. Man is similar to God, but man is not identical to God, for there is only One Immutable God without a second, unborn and uncaused.

The mind of writer, for example Dickens, exists within his characters. His characters represent what existed in his mind, but, while his characters may be said to be Dickens, yet Dickens is not identical with his characters.

To borrow from a Hermetic teaching and using the Law of Correspondence: "THE ALL is in man and yet man is far from being THE ALL. Yet, The ALL is immanent in man and in every particle that goes to make up man. Can there be any greater mystery than this of "All in THE ALL; and THE ALL in All?"[52]

---

52 The Kybalion, Three Initiates

Until man realizes the Self, the existence of the One Life within his being, the truth which is the source of universality will elude him. God is beyond self-existence, beyond infinite and beyond eternal.

The Buddha realized this which allowed him to say: "Gate gate para gate para sam gate bodhi swaha." What does this mean? Translated it is: "Gone, gone, gone to the other shore, beyond. O what an awakening, all hail!" It is a beautiful and poetic prayer of the acceptance of truth of the divine within oneself. The Buddha, once a human being like you and I, is now a universal bodhisattva.

Each human being who thus returns to God with this realization actually expands and enriches the Spirit of each soul within The Infinite All.

In the process of evolution a human being evolves through thought choices. The sages know that man must make choices, but they also know that man is not aware of the his universal nature due to lack of development in consciousness, that the unity of the whole lives within man. This means, of course, that man is never separated from his true nature, even though he thinks he is.

A human being can never be a completely independent organism, because man's true nature is inseparably united with the whole. As the sloka at the beginning states only man alone thinks of himself as separate. Separateness is purely imaginary and illusory. Therefore, egoism is the greatest violation of the Law of Universality and produces the most disastrous results, say the Great Ones.

Man is a soul with a physical body. Using the Law of Analogy, man is also the universal soul with a universal body. The difference is one of form, scale and consciousness. Man is the universe in the form of a seed. Man is also the the finished product of that seed.

The mentality of the sages of ancient Egypt understood this. In the last century, after a deep fifteen year study of the Temple of Amon-Re in Luxor, Egypt, R.A.Schwaller de Lubicz realized the fundamental thought behind the fiat lux: "Let There be Light". He wrote: "Man as he is, whatever our opinion may be of his imperfection or perfection, represents for us the ultimate organically living product of the universe. It is not a question of microcosm alongside macrocosm, but of the universe incarnate in man - man the anthropocosm. We are therefore able to know, by sensation, intellectually, and intuitively, all that is innate in ourselves, what we unconsciously are. And consciousness of what we are can be awakened at certain moments."[53]

The Christ said two thousand years ago: "I and my Father are one", John 10:30. He did not say I am God or I am the Father. The universe is in man, just as the tree is in the seed.

This law is at the heart of the anthropocosm doctrine and is based on the principle that de Lubicz alluded to above, that every seed is a synthesis of what it will produce and what it produces will be the symbol of the synthesis, which the appearance, the symbol can evoke. Simply put, man and universe are a synthesis, but to realize this is another matter.

The sense of synthesis, wholeness or universality cannot be described, but it is real and it can be known through what the Teacher DK calls the final stage of illumination. The unfoldment of the intuition, what the ancient Egyptian sages

---

[53] The Intelligence of the Heart, R.A. Schwaller de Lubicz, 1956, Lecture given to Congress of Symbolists in Paris.

called the "intelligence of the heart", leads to this ultimate stage of illumination.

In the new era, the the Masters will revive the use of symbols and the symbolic method of the ancient mystery schools in fresh new ways, to awaken the spiritual faculty of the intuition or intelligence of the heart. This will be largely brought about through meditative methods. In "reading" a symbol, it must always be remembered that the interpretation is always representative of each person's unfolding.

In reality, there is no distinction between universal man and individual man. One is the reflection of the other at different stages of consciousness. An example from geometry is the circle: How can one separate the circumference and the center of the circle? Without a center there is no circle and without a circle there is no center. One implies the other.

This is where most of the problems within humanity have arisen. Man is not separate from the universe nor can he be divided from it. The One is irreducible. "I and my Father are one" were Christ's words as mentioned above, and He extended the truth further when He said: "When you pray, pray to the Christ of God; include yourself as the Christ."

The Law of Universality allows for rebirth can be transcended. If there is a light placed in the center of a dark room, (the darkness representing ignorance) the best way to reach that light is to go straight to it. Why circle around it [reincarnate] again, after again, after again? The teachings of the great ones say, to go directly to that light, pick it up and incorporate it, be the light and then you are done with all the darkness and reincarnation.

It is only in the failure to go directly to the central point that the Law of Rebirth is in motion. The mind that accepts and realizes the central fact of the soul, the inner Christ, arrives at the center and all the going round and round will cease and come to an end. The limitless beauty and life of the universe awaits all who discover the essence of this law.

Universality states that there is both individualized consciousness and synthesis simultaneously. Each of us is a oneness, expressing the synthetic whole as an individualized unit of wholeness according to one's state of consciousness.

To awaken the sense of universality, a senior member of the spiritual Hierarchy asks that the spiritual seeker reflect on the following question and verse:

> *"What is the relationship, of yourself to the universe?"*
>
> *"The language of the heart is universal.*
> *Brotherly love is best understood*
> *through the unification of heart and soul.*
> *Honor the God Presence within,*
> *and each person as a child of God.*
> *Truly all are related in the Cosmos*
> *from whence thee came,*
> *and to whence thee shall return."*[54]

22. LAW OF GROUP DHARMA

This is an Aquarian law associated with the dharma of groups and group will, and not individual will, as expressed through the Plan. It is a new area of group commitment and discipline. It is a recognition by those in the 5th Kingdom of Souls (the spiritual

Hierarchy) of group response and activity in their physical plane groups of aspirants and disciples.

This activity began nearly eighty years ago, with the work of the Tibetan Teacher DK and his amanuensis Alice A. Bailey. It has spread since to the four corners of the world. To date, group experiments in small numbers are growing as the new era unfolds. It must be understood that each group has its dharma or duty and all have their peculiar objective.

Dharma is living justly, in harmony with the life of the soul, spiritual truth and the Plan. It is the pursuit of all avenues of spiritual development with the goal of embodying and manifesting a spiritual culture and civilization. It is working with one's karma in such as way as to balance it while allowing for the unfolding of soul consciousness. Dharma is a balancer of karma.

Unbalanced karma is more rapidly transformed when a group point of tension is achieved, a group tension, not of conflict, but of the group holding a focussed recognition of their alignment with the forces of light, and the task at hand. This brings about evolutionary group transformation and greater service to the Plan.

This law is connected with the Law of Service and bolstered by the Law of Detachment and Laws of Soul Life. The fulfillment of dharma becomes the motivating factor of the heart, both in the individual and the group. This is a development of the sense of responsibility that first appeared in the awakening of the soul, in the heart of a human being.

In the new groups, students clarify and relate their individual dharma to the group responsibility. When there is group cohesiveness, right action can be taken, accompanied as much as possible by detachment, so that that group members are not constantly preoccupied with dharma. When dharma flows naturally and is not forced, the best work is done.

A disciple is a title that each person earns by applying the teachings of spiritual transformation, while solving problems with reason, clear thinking, love and understanding. In group work, in the process of purification, personality obstacles such as self-centeredness or self-pride are more easily exposed for transformation.

The will to group integration is hard work as it occurs simultaneously, internally, in relationship and in activity. It is hard work, but as the veils of glamor, personality habits and obstacles are shed like the old skin of a snake, the wisdom gained of experience becomes the new skin, more brilliant than before. Spiritual blindness, lack of honesty, pride and lack of self-sacrifice are the greatest obstacles on the path of discipleship to groups.

Acceptance of responsibility for one's karma, non-blaming, willingness to transmute personality weaknesses, taking responsibility for one's thoughts, words and actions, making sure each step one takes is purer than the one before, treating others with love and understanding, are qualities the Master looks for in aspirants and disciples who wish to serve the Plan.

Dharma is taking responsibility for that aspect of karma of a particular world cycle and includes the individual karma of those involved in its fulfillment. The disciple takes responsibility for his or her part and works accordingly for its right fulfillment. He or she begins to understand dharma, as seen by the Masters, and does his or her part in the transmutation of world karma.

One must think in the broader terms of humanity itself, and thus bring the quality of group relationship into expression. Group relationship is an emerging spiritual quality of group activity. Questions such as "Will my action tend to the group good?" "Will the group suffer or hurt if I do this action?" are a reflection of this quality. The cosmic Ray of Harmony will support the spiritual quality of group relationship, and enable the *Will-to-Good*[55] to be turned for the best advantage.

The word 'relationship' will gradually become part of humanity's consciousness and our civilization will adjust itself to new conditions of goodwill and right relationship. All aspects of the life of God are interdependent, and when one proceeds consciously to fuller expression, all benefit.

The activity of the will that flows from soul consciousness will create a refusal to contact any vibration deemed inimical to the group life. "In the new era for humankind, the ability to use new energies and mechanisms as a result of contact with Higher Intelligence will need to be performed with absolute responsibility towards the Cosmic Law. All those who are pioneers of the new age will need to understand what being a new human means and the changes it requires in consciousness, attitudes and behavior toward one other. The unfolding new era will be one of Freedom in which groups and centers of energy will be emerging in greater numbers. It must be remembered that the new energies of Love, Light and Truth cannot abide where law is

broken or in old wineskins. All who would be of the New Age cannot break laws and remain in the presence of these New Age energies."[56] This is the essence of the the the Law of Dharma—to live in right relationship with the higher law, peacefully, lovingly and with respect for the freedom of all beings.

Such is the nature of this law which is not opposed to freedom or harmful to life, but exists for the glorification of what the heart of humanity has always sought. If each one acts according to the commandments of the heart, the actions of the group can do no harm.

This law was first introduced by Helena Roerich in her writings on Living Ethics. Helena Roerich was the amanuensis of Master Morya. She and Master Morya collaborated on the Agni Yoga book series, to prepare individuals for group work and Hierarchical cooperation. The teachings on Living Ethics are scattered throughout the Agni Yoga books. Living Ethics has four basic principles:

1. Carrying within one's heart the fiery energy of Agni, love infused with higher will.
2. Alignment with the consciousness of the soul and the Kingdom of Souls.
3. Responsible, directed loving thought.
4. The realization that the evolution of the planetary consciousness is a pressing necessity.

Planetary consciousness is a planet united in purpose and goodness. It is an attainable aspiration for all, and each person has an opportunity to play a role in it, according to one's unique aptitudes. This is a law that

---

[55] a divine quality of will, discussed later, that imparts to the Purpose and the Plan, warmth and magnetic appeal. It is redemptive and healing in nature.

[56] Revelation, Birth of a New Age, David Spangler

places group relationship in right relationship with the potency of energies that will be available in the new age. It is incumbent upon each person who seeks to live in the new age, to live with spiritual love. Each person can begin by not setting oneself up to oppose or be against this or that, because the spiritual principles of love and oneness runs throughout the higher laws.

This law teaches that to live in a just world all have to share in making the world just, not just individually but also in the sharing of group dharma, that specific dharma the group has come into manifestation for. For example, to balance world karma, dissipate world glamor or to work with any of the twelve branches of the new world model, based upon the the cosmic zodiacal pattern of twelve.

Eventually planetary consciousness will be the expression of one great act of living faithful service. Eventually it will be will of the soul, guided by love that will express through the Plan. This is the goal of our planetary Logos for humanity in the new era.

Th following Vedic prayer, the *Gayatri*, is considered a pillar of the Law of Dharma:

"Oh Thou Who givest sustenance to the universe, From Whom all things proceed, to Whom all things return, Unveil to us the face of the true spiritual Sun, that we may know the truth and do our whole duty, as we journey to Thy sacred feet."
(The Teacher DK's adaption)

23. *LAWS OF MANIFESTATION*

This law which is a plurality, because of the many ways it work, has nothing to do with magic, finance or faith. It has to do with the laws of manifestation as it will work out in the new era. It will still deal with the translation of energy from one level or state to another but with an added provision. It will deal with the processes of releasing the potential of the soul and the expression of divinity. In other words, manifesting what already exists, primarily the divine potential of the soul within humanity.

The workings of the laws of manifestation will become more visible as the human mind comes into resonance with the spiritual Hierarchy and the Christ. One of Christ's roles is to oversee the process of the spiritual Hierarchy coming into outer manifestation as the World Teacher.

Christ will reframe the laws of manifestation for human understanding in the light of the emergence of the soul. Each stage in the attainment of a higher consciousness manifests a slightly different reality. Each stage must be experienced to know its progressively unfolding reality.

In the coming era, moving from a lower to a higher level on the "ladder" of consciousness will be seen as part of the manifestation process. This includes the the lower kingdoms, the Fifth Kingdom and our planetary Logos.

There is nothing mysterious or esoteric about the essential nature of manifestation. It is a simple, though complex process. But, to work with the energies of the new era, requires a dynamic state of consciousness attuned to the soul.

Humans manifest all the time through their very lives and choices. Humanity has always manifested. It just has not manifested in alignment with the inner divine pattern.

As mentioned earlier, this law is plural, because the level of existence it operates on, determines which aspect of the law is activated. In the simplest terms, physical energy brings about the physical things of life. Emotional energy brings about desired conditions in one's environment. Mental energy brings about an integration of the personality in that the mind controls and uses the emotional and physical levels of energy to manifest, even though it operates from a sense of separateness and ego.

An integrated personality is a rung away from understanding the deeper application of this law—that of personality and soul integration and expression. The first rung is called the birth of the Christ in the heart. The attitude of "getting things" is replaced by the need to transform consciousness so that what is felt in the heart becomes manifest. There is a saying, "when the student is ready...." It is then that synchronicities manifest that support spiritual growth in the student's life.

The second rung brings with it a growing awareness of the soul. It is the purifying or transforming work, for which the individual has taken responsibility. Previously, for the separative ego, the basic need was to acquire. For the personality becoming soul-infused, the motivation comes from seeing a vision of a greater whole.

There is a new yet ancient principle of manifestation: "Form follows consciousness". An example is that when consciousness in resonance with a higher level of consciousness, forms manifest accordingly. It must be kept in mind that wherever one's consciousness aims, the vital or etheric body follows.

Imagine soul-infused consciousness merging with vibrations of light and beings on higher levels of consciousness, amplified and directed. In the new world of light and energy, one can understand why the workings of the laws of manifestation will be important.

Since the new age is also a new level of consciousness, any description of it would be inadequate. What can be said is that it will be world where new levels of consciousness will create new forms for the working out and restoring of the Plan.

The Master Teachers emphasize the importance of understanding that a new world must be created in cooperation with the consciousness of humanity, and that the new world will not be a completely finished product, but one that is in the process of manifesting. It needs to be noted that in the early stages of the shift, soul consciousness may not be much in evidence, but that will change.

The Teacher DK says in A Treatise On White Magic by Alice A. Bailey, "As a man dwells upon the nature of his soul, he becomes like that soul. His thought is focussed in the soul consciousness and he becomes that soul in manifestation through the medium of the personality."

Many times Teachers will ask their students: "Where do you put your attention?" They go on to tell those who are making soul contact to avoid the tendency to be judgmental. This attitude only serves to feed criticism that makes the individual's efforts counter-productive and inadequate to the task. Oneness flows through all the laws and the attitude of one's attention should be to see beyond the form, and recognize the soul or light within all forms.

In the new era, the creative power of consciousness will finally be realized by humanity. The function of the soul in the new will be to express balanced good, truth, right relationship, and a just world with love and beauty. Humanity will also realize the differences between personality and soul manifestation. The latter unfolds divinity from within while the former attracts to itself from without to satisfy the personality.

Once humanity is established in the new age, in cooperation with the Christ, it will safely be able tap into the potent energies manifestation and learn how to use the will constructively.

The more we know of the methods of this law, the better able we shall be to take advantage of the available energies for the manifestation of "heaven on earth".

"Our aim is to manifest the kingdom of heaven on earth, to manifest perfection, to manifest the new heaven, the new earth, an age of abundance, of plenty, of beauty, harmony, law, order, and above all, LOVE"[57]

24. *LAW OF THE CHRISTOS*

This law governs and controls how and when the Holy Spirit, the Shekina or the Divine Presence of God pours into the worlds of form. Christos is a spiritual title meaning "Christ-Bearer", one who carries the light and love of the great Christos—a Son of God, and reveals it.

It is through the Christos that the Shekina can flow. The Presence of God has been spoken of by the Teacher DK, as the fourth divine quality that is behind the Divine Will, Love and Intelligence. It is this fourth quality of "presence" that brings the "peace that passeth understanding". It is the Christos that makes the peace of God knowable.

Christ in man is the indwelling Logos, the wisdom of God incarnate. This is the potential inherent in man which this law reveals. The Christos is the mediating force between the Father and His creation. One of the "jobs" of the indwelling Christ (the soul of a human being), is to keep the body and mind in proper balance with each other and itself. This coms into play as the personality's recognition of the soul and the universal love principle increases.

The essence of this law is the Christ Consciousness of non-dual oneness. This law exists to create or restore that divine state of sanity of the mind, so that the "peace that passeth understanding", can begin to function. Insanity is the antithesis of sanity, and presence is their synthesis. As Heaven wills, the Law of the Christos guides and directs the revelation of "presence" in the world.

As stated in Galatians 3:28: "There is neither slave nor free, male nor female, nor angel, nor human...". This non-duality is more than the harmony of opposites. It is their essential non-separateness. Love is the realization of the unity that underlies all creation and it is this aspect of divine love that allows the soul, the inner Christ to be a vehicle for presence in the world.

It is this law, as just mentioned which guides the revealing presence of God—that all pervasive field of unity that underlies the polarity of Father, spirit and Mother, matter. It is through the Christ Consciousness that the glory and radiance of God as Father-Spirit and Mother-Matter is revealed.

It is this law which brings one into a relationship with the presence of God. This law will operate more fully in the new dispensation as the process of initiation is established, so that humanity may work in harmony with the Christ, the Masters of the

---

[57] Laws of Manifestation, David Spangler

spiritual Hierarchy, and Beings who share the will, love and light of God.

In the the ancient Egyptian temple schools, called at that time the Temples of Isis-Chrestos (chrestos meaning goodness) the neophyte, having been accepted, took the oath of a chrestian, to study and apply the lesser mysteries and submit to the arduous task of self-transformation and purification that leads to the greater mysteries of the Christos with its portal of initiation.

In the new era, the Christos energy emanating from the Christ and externalized Masters will nurture the soul into full flowering. That, and chrestians passing though the new group oriented chrestian curriculum of service and self-transformation, which will prepare the chrestian for the portal of initiation.

Helena P. Blavatsky wrote of the Chrestian and Christos mystery teachings in The Secret Doctrine. The terms Christos and chrestos, both predate Christianity. They were terms used in the days of Atlantis. A chrestos is a disciple of the good preparing for the transfiguration initiation. The chrestos passing through trials of purification undergoes the transfiguration of light and enters into the greater mysteries, later emerging as a Christos.

In the symbology of the Mystery Temple, Christos meant that the path had been taken and the Holy Grail reached. The Christos is a power present within the heart of every human being that has the power to transfigure the world. A Christos is this law in embodiment.

In the age of Pisces, which is ending, a Christos of great spiritual stature came as the World Savior whose work was to show the way of love, of transformation of desire into sacrifice and of the transformation of

individual will into spiritual will. In the new age of Aquarius, this same Christos comes as the World Teacher whose work is to bring humanity closer to God through the unfolding of group or soul consciousness. He who is the Aquarian Christos or World Teacher is he who is also, the Eldest Brother of humanity.

The role of the coming World Teacher is multi-faceted:

1. To nourish the life of the human soul, to nurture the awakening soul to full bloom, and to lead humanity to the Light of God.

2. Oversee the instructing chrestians and initiates in such a form, so that the Hierarchy can be drawn closer to the planetary source of Will, Shamballa, and humanity blend with the planetary source of Love, Hierarchy.

3. He will be the great teacher of Karma and as the word of God incarnate, he will lead the souls of humanity to liberation from the great wheel of rebirth.

The Teacher DK says that there is a fourth task that is being revealed to humanity regarding the role of the Christ in the new era: Christ will speed up the apparatus of the soul, and prepare humanity for the coming of a great One from Sirius, who is waiting for the exact moment.

Sirius, the brightest star in the sky has a long standing relationship with the Earth. It radiates a brilliant light and has evolved to express the "peace which passeth understanding". It is a binary star system that astronomers have observed is moving closer to our solar system and now speculate a third star, Sirius C. There is a relationship between Sirius and this law.

The Law of the Christos diminishes polarities. It reconciles 'yes' and 'no', right and wrong, good and evil, and brings the concepts of good and evil into non-dual resolution of synthesis. It rules with the balancing power of goodness and perfection. It exists so that evolving humanity may attain Christ-like perfection.

The Christ is also an office. The Teacher DK says in Externalization of the Hierarchy by Alice A. Bailey: "When I say the department of the Christ, I would remind you that the name "Christ" is that of an office—an office that has always had its Head. I do not mention the Christ or the Buddha as among these Avatars because They are Avatars of another class and of infinitely greater potency." It is important to keep this distinction in mind and that Avatars are always associated with the office of the Christ.

The Office of the Christ and Beings associated with it, are guided by ten guiding principles:[58]

1. We live in an open-ended universe of free will, part of the myriad universes that make up the Universal Mind. Unless an evolutionary program shows an opening for spiritual programming, the Office of the Christ does not interfere.
2. Our local universe has at its center and is guided by a more evolved pattern of life known as the Higher Evolution.
3. The identification of individual will with God's Will and all-encompassing love allows for multi-dimensional overlap and cooperation with spiritual brotherhoods, which is essential for the continued evolution of consciousness.
4. The privilege of working with the three great Orders of the universe comes from alignment with the great Law of Sacrifice.
5. Resonance between the consciousness of humanity and higher evolutionary levels is necessary for attunement with Universal Intelligence.
6. A Christ perfected individual is part of a greater continuum of consciousness that deals with creating a continuum of different levels of consciousness.
7. In the perfection of the Christ Consciousness, the spiritualized human being has available for acquisition, five higher bodies of light that allow him or her to be an integral part of the work of salvation.
8. A soul that has mastered the Science and Light, can cooperate with the Order of Enoch.
9. Planets passing though electromagnetic null-zone cycles of stars and galaxies can have their evolutionary programs accelerated. Null zones allow space-time overlap of different dimensions, allowing for spiritual transformation to occur through exposure to higher consciousness realms Light.
10. As stars, planets and solar systems pass through null zone thresholds and cycles, they undergo a transition from one density of light to a higher density of light using spiritually advanced means of inter-dimensional-interstellar transference, with the free will of life forms always honored.

This is the law which operates for the salvation and redemption of worlds and would not be possible were it not for the

---

great sacrifice of the Son of God upon the Cosmic Cross of Matter.

"I Am the Christos within you.
I Am the Presence within you.
In every action and interaction towards the Light, Through every circumstance and every encounter When fortitude is most lacking.

You and I are not different. Remove the veils that entrap you. There is no time, we shall tread the Path together.
Let not the realm of darkness consume you.

You and I are of the Father's Perfection, Light, Life and Glory. Be the light dwelling in Light.
Be the presence dwelling in Presence. Let whoever hears and can see arise from slumber.

Embrace the light, love and presence flowing from the realm of Spirit, Guiding you into the Age of Light. It shall accelerate the path of soul awakening that leads to the state of Christ Consciousness.

Let whoever hears and can see arise!

Glory to Thee, Logos! Glory to Thee, Grace! Glory to Thee, Holy Spirit! Glory to Thee, Glory!"
- A Gnostic Prayer (adapted)

25. LAW OF EVOLUTION

This great law which provide a breathtaking view of evolution, is concerned with the perfection of form expression, and with the evolution of the form aspect as it is gradually adapted to be an exponent or an expression of consciousness. Consciousness evolves under the Law of Love, the law which governs our solar system.

This law considers the cosmos as a vibrant field of consciousness seeking to manifest its potential. In this solar system's previous 'manvantara'[59], it was the Law of Economy which governed the intelligence of matter aspect of divinity. With the Law of economy we will not here deal nor with the Law of Being, scheduled for this solar system's next incarnation. Our focus is on the Law of Love, the evolutionary law that governs for this manvantara.

Keep in mind that evolution proceeds through incalculable cycles or evolutionary thresholds with their unique qualities of dimension and consciousness, a fact that becomes self-evident through the expansion of consciousness. This is the law behind the gradual unfolding of spirit through matter through various stages of consciousness.

This law has lead to the complexity of forms and to the evolution of life forms with free will - that unique gift that enables the individualized will to work towards spiritual destiny, or not.

The development of self-consciousness separateness is a necessary stage, but it must now must be superseded by soul or group consciousness, the next stage of development. Without it, cooperation with the spiritual Hierarchy, part of the unfolding plan of God, would not be possible.

Beyond soul or group consciousness is a stage called synthesis or the pure consciousness of spirit, which is necessary to cooperate with the divine will and higher of a planetary Logos. Synthesis under a Logos governed by the most high Law of Being.

---

[59] A Sanskrit term for a period of incalculable duration. Our solar system is in the second of three great cycles.

In the new earth, this law will concern the evolution of the soul actively working with the Office of the Christ. A higher vibratory frequency of the Law of Love radiates through the galactic sector into which our solar system is moving.

Nothing stops the flow of evolution until it is finished, though a human being can slowly go with it, or delay or speed up his/her own evolution. With the advance of consciousness, a soul-infused humanity will becoming aware of the body's etheric envelope and that it is shaped by one's thoughts and feelings. Energy follows thought and form follows consciousness.

There are presently three types of human beings on the planet. In very general terms they are:

1. Soul that have incarnated on earth for the experience of personality development. This is a necessary stage of human development where selfishness is served. It is where the light of matter rules. It must be remembered that loss or failure is experienced in thought, not in the consciousness of the soul, and that thought emanates from consciousness. From the perspective of the soul, there is no judgement, failure or loss. The wheel of rebirth rules.

2. Human beings awakening to the light of the soul. It manifest as sensitivity to the light of higher aspiration, a stimulation coming from the soul. It is in this stage that the waning of the personality and the waxing of the soul begins. It is a battleground of spirit vs. matter, and choice. Though painful and full of suffering, the soul experiences the process not from the personality level, but from the higher spiritual perspective of consciousness and the laws. Support comes in from the wheel of life.

3. The human being is living a directed life towards soul consciousness, to expressing the qualities of the soul, and becoming aware that higher laws are at work. They see the personality as a vehicle for service, allowing the soul to express greater soul life and work with the divine plan. These souls are rare but increasing in number. The wheel of rebirth is nearing its end.

In the new era of light, humanity will continue its evolution, where it will be the common good, the good of the world that will orient the life of individuals towards group relationships. The energy of goodness will flow through groups, funneled into the world for certain constructive purposes.

The Teacher DK in Letters on Occult Meditation says: "When the right time comes, The spiritual Hierarchy will be able to use these groups as focal points for Their activities. When soul alignment is better grasped and when groups in physical incarnation can work in real cooperation, then the 'Nirmanakayas' (a Buddhist term for beings of great wisdom) will be able to act with great force upon the evolutions found thereon." Basically, soul alignment furthers the evolution of humanity and its access to available spiritual energies.

One point should be remembered about the two types of forces, since all is dual in nature. There are both forces of good and forces of evil. The former are dedicated to the beneficent task of purifying and assisting all lives in the three worlds of material evolution and to the liberation of the soul in form, and the latter to the retardation of the Plan of God, and to the continuous strengthening of matter so as to keep the soul a prisoner in dense matter.

While both groups work with energy, their motives and objectives widely differ. The forces of good works with the expansion of consciousness and the energies spiritual love, light and will. The forces of evil work with the distortion and manipulation of truth, the energies of fear, illusion, deception, jealousy, etc. to keep man thinking himself as separate from God, with no true understanding of the God principle or why man has free will.

Evil seeks to contract consciousness into form. Good seeks to expand consciousness into spirit. The main task of the spiritual Hierarchy has ever been to stand between the forces of evil and humanity, to bring imperfection into the light so that evil can find no place for action, and to keep the door open into the spiritual realm. Evil itself is but an illusion. But, until humanity realizes that the domination of spirit (and its reflection, the soul) by matter is what constitutes evil, The Hierarchy's safeguarding of the light will be necessary.

At no time does the spiritual Hierarchy infringe upon the natural processes of evolutionary growth or the normally slow development of the various kingdoms in nature towards divine expression. But, they will take advantage of every opportunity while always acting in harmony with the purpose of the planetary Logos and divine law.

God thought two universal planes of consciousness into being: the One and the Other, the spiritual and its manifestation. "The heavens and the earth, created He them" (Genesis). God's spiritual universe remains in a harmonious state, while the other can fall into states of disharmony

activating the laws to bring conditions into harmony.

It is important to note that humanity through soul unfoldment will be in the position of understanding the creative process of evolution. The soul and its incarnated self are gradually getting closer and closer together. Their unification is the goal of the Planetary Logos for humanity in this next evolutionary cycle of Aquarius.

Earth is a school of unique spiritual development that revolves around love and service. The Earth school is one of the most sought after by souls for the opportunity to contribute. As the earth moves into a higher, more refined field of light, the opportunity to serve and contribute will be magnified ten fold. It will provide souls the opportunity to experience new degrees of the Christ consciousness and ways in which to demonstrate the soul in form.

In the new era, the expansion of soul consciousness will not be limited as it is now. The coordinated efforts of orders of Higher Intelligence will pour their light into the world and in return humanity will have the opportunity to outpour into the universe for the good of the whole.

The new era will provide a process that allows the soul and its vehicle, the personality to progress for better cooperation with the higher intelligences of the universe. The greatest catalyst for spiritual growth is LIGHT. Light throws the forces of evil into confusion.

At this present time what is most needed from humanity is a welcoming vibration will evoke a response from the Christ. The more one understands the three recognitions, the sooner will this invocative vibration spring forth from the heart of humanity. It is the expression of soul-ness in time and space that creates a magnetic pull on the forces of good, which brings up the subject of time, space and being in relation to this law.

Time, Space and Being are the universal main actors in evolution. The phenomenon known as time has permeated collective consciousness. of humanity on this planet. The phenomenon of linear time has kept humanity shackled to the material plane. In the new era human beings will not experience passing through time but experiencing definite regions of space and consciousness. What this means is Fifth Dimensional soul consciousness will change how time and space are experienced, since consciousness will become the generator of movement.

Time, Space and Being is a trinitized creation of Infinite Mind and each of these three aspects of Mind are dual. Time is split into past and present; Space is split into here and there, and Being is split into tangible matter and intangible spirit. Matter is spirit or energy in a condensed state, but it is the energy in matter which is of significance in terms of evolution. Duality is necessary for Infinite Mind to manifest and Spirit to evolve through the process of genesis.

Time, Space and Being are not separate entities from the perspective of Universal Mind. They only appear to human perception as three separate entities, and as here and there, the present and past, and as physical and spiritual. Time in its absolute nature is the eternal now. Space in its absolute nature is immeasurable as static neutral energy. Being in its absolute nature is the synthesis of all potential. Pondering on their absolute natures will reveal much in terms of their relationships and correspondences.

Linear time exists where there are condensed physical forms of energy. As the physical forms evolve and their density changes due to the transformation of consciousness so does the experience of time, space and being. The experience of time, space and being by Fourth and Fifth Dimensional entities will be different because their consciousness is different. Consciousness dictates the experience.

In the new era, a second of time or thousands of years will lose their meaning and as such, what marks time will be experienced non-linearly. Being will be experienced as a living presence permeating the universe. Space will no longer be seen as filled with nothing, but as filled with living energy as humanity's new senses and bodies will register all kinds of new spatial phenomena.

New ways of experiencing and experimenting with Time, Space and Being as entities, will result in the further unfolding of the soul in form.

The experience of Time, Space and Being in the new era, will no longer be the limiting illusions that they currently are. They will be experienced from within the continuum of consciousness. It is the shifting from personality identification to that of the soul, that will further expand humanity's capacity to experience higher levels of reality. Thus, humanity will be equipped to participate in a greater part of the wholeness of life.

Etheric-physical bodies will be more sensitive to the previously unknown realities which fill space. Communication will be experienced telepathically with thoughts propelled by love and speeds faster than light. The "physicality" of form due to the etheric nature of the New Earth will express more of the qualities of Fifth Dimensional light, color and sound.

The Teacher DK in Telepathy and the Etheric Vehicle by Alice A. Bailey, says that "Space is an Entity", and like the universe, a living organism. What this could be interpreted as meaning is that Space is the static essence of the pure intelligence of the Infinite Creative Mind which knows all and everything. The fact is that man can conceive of Time, Space and Being as absolute entities, and DK gos on to say that the glory of man lies in this fact. Evolution leads man to his destiny, but evolution also honors free will.

Man is a being with a creative spirit in form. Being is the expression of energy as eternal limitless life. In the New Earth, man will have an etheric-physical form that allows for greater soul unfoldment. Christ has said that He is bringing"more abundant life" to humanity. This has been humankind's birthright since the dawn of creation.

Though bent on destruction and ignorant of God, man has shown the courage to change course. God know what is in every heart and even though God know that He alone is the cause, yet God's wrath is never aroused. It is God's love for humanity drives the evolutionary process, that tears the shroud and brings man back through birth and re-birth into the light. There is a poetic verse that goes: "Man plays the fool...then I applaud. I make the tool sharper to My Eternal Cause"[60].

To understand this poetic words is to understand that God works in such a way that all things work together for good. If words such as these evoke higher thoughts or emotions for the way in which life works, then its words have done their job. Love is the greatest power in the universe for evolution, and for evoking out of life more harmony, peace and above all greater opportunities to participate in the life of the living cosmos.

Every human being is a center of eternal limitless life and a point of consciousness through which God experiences and understands everything from the individual's point of view and responds through His Cosmic Laws according to one's unfolding.

This is why there is no one right answer or interpretation to a question or a symbol. This is why there is such diversity of expression in form. Man is the result of the One Uncaused First Cause, created by Spirit and from Spirit, whose nature is Eternal Love, Wisdom, Perfection and Goodness, with the power of free will. Present man is a stage in the evolutionary process of MAN. There is no limit to man's evolutionary potential as the Spirit which created man is limitless.

Humanity must learn to use free will with wisdom and love and is given the freedom to choose the path that leads towards self-realization and unity with the divine and beyond or not. Each individual's evolution contributes to the evolution of the whole. Evolution is the divine play of progressive manifestation. Evolution moves in a spiral of ascending order, not a circle, with each turn representing a higher octave of love.

"The plough of God is accomplishing its work, making everything come to the surface, the good and the bad, the past and the future. Our material civilization will soon be giving way to a more spiritual culture. The best is yet to be." These are the words of the Teacher DK in Esoteric Healing by Alice A. Bailey. May His words encourage us to

---

[60] Messages From the Golden Density, George W. Van Tassel.

continue with the transformation of the ego and plough the ground for preparation into the new era. When faced with a limiting situation or overcoming, recall or quietly declare:

"I am not bound to any false idea. I, with Spirit, inhabit Eternity and Limitlessness. The Divine order of God's universe is manifest in my mind and in all my affairs."
-Gnostic Prayer (adapted)

26. *LAW OF RECOGNITION*

The term 'recognition' as used by the Teacher DK through the books of Alice A. Bailey, means in simple words, the ability to recognize that inner state of consciousness—the light within our fellow travelers, kindred souls and those enlightened ones who serve.

It is a law connected with the spiritual ideas of liberty, equality and brotherhood, and is laying the foundation for the coming civilization. It brings forth new mode of thinking and helped produce the Magna Carta and French Revolution, the ending of slavery, the Atlantic Charter, the Four Freedoms, the Bill of Rights, the Universal Declaration of Human Rights, the development of International Human Rights Law, and more recently the Bangkok Declaration.

The Will-to-Good of Shamballa is the driving force within this law which is the recognition of the soul and its goodness, expressing itself as practical goodwill through individuals, in communities and among nations. It is a law which supports a just world baed on balance and equality.

This law only begins to function in one's life only at a certain stage of the path, as it is based on a capacity inherent in the life of the soul. Therefore, the more the shift of

identity is to the soul, the easier it will be to recognize that all human beings are children of the one Father and that all men are brothers. At the same time, the more one is committed to recognizing the light - looking for it, waiting for it, believing in it - the more a human being recognizes him/herself as a soul.

The more this identification with the soul is practiced, the more effective the result will be: realization that one already possesses the desired inner state. It is a kind of living meditation that facilitates identification with the true and genuine self.

The Law of Recognition deals with the nature of divinity that is latent within the human being to be contacted and unfolded. One can only see what is one's self; The eye cannot see what the mind has not registered. If we do not see aspects of life, it is because those aspects are undeveloped and latent within one's self.

To illustrate: one does not see the divine in his brother because the divine in one's self is not yet contacted and known; the form aspect and its limitations are so developed that the soul remains hidden. A person who is only aware of his brother's form does not see the soul.

The practice of recognition sensitizes the heart to the soul. The latent soul faculty when developed will reveal a new reality of existence. The hidden powers of the soul brought to full expression will make a person aware of a scheme of life and being hitherto unrecognized, because not seen.

The practice of meditation or a daily practice of recognition is very effective in developing capacity for recognition, but sadly, is not practiced by enough of humanity. This type of recognition has nothing to do with receiving recognition for work done. The Masters do not get recognition for the work done by their disciples, though They initiated the original impulse. So to, should groups work seeking no recognition and without attachment to results. What is only asked of group's, is a united recognition of the scope of the endeavor and a united striving completely absorbed in service.

Natural to the human condition is the suffering which arises from emotional and mental conflict, wounded pride, anger, failed relationships or goals, clash of ideals and so on—a result of attachment to the personality. The solution is recognition of a reasoned approach to life through soul unfoldment which transcends self-centeredness and viewpoints.

The continuation of human evolution relies on recognition of the Three Recognitions mentioned earlier and again here: the Soul, the Kingdom of Souls and the Divine Plan. Members of the Fifth Kingdom or Kingdom of Souls passed through the experience of being a member of the Human Kingdom. This enables the planetary Logos to develop the capacity for recognition of higher levels of reality.

The laws that govern spiritual progress are universal. The laws respond to the unfolding consciousness. The laws are continuously interacting with life. The members of the spiritual Hierarchy are proof of humanity's potential. Recognition of this provides hope, trust, assurance, aspiration and inspiration in the spiritual path.

The self-centered personality recognizes the three worlds of physical, emotional and mental reality as that which can can best serve itself, creating patterns of selfishness and greed. The heart that is sensitized by

pain and suffering opens the mind to the possibility of the soul's existence.

It is a fact that the forces of Light are more powerful than the forces that seek to thwart the Light. The forces opposed to the Light do not recognize this fact. But until a human being recognizes that light is stronger than darkness, there will be the temptation to submit to fear.

The personality's non-recognition of the soul is in no way a judgment, for each stage of development has its place. But as soon as human being opens to the possibility of a higher consciousness, this power of recognition is activated. Even meditation of the word 'Recognition', since words are living things, will open the door to inspiration.

To participate in the creation of a new world, there should be recognition of those ideas and ideals on which the new world will be based. The new world of the soul with its ideas and ideals is already finding expression in human affairs. Three examples are:

1. Those voices in the world speaking out for justice, brotherhood, and equality.
2. Those committed to transcending conflict and fostering cooperation. Outlines of the evolutionary direction toward unity and wholeness are becoming manifest in the achievements of organizations and groups.
3. The world of cyberspace which has emerged can be likened to the etheric web of the planet. What passes through both the electronic planetary web and the etheric web is energy corresponding to different qualities or grades of consciousness. The current consciousness of humanity dictates the need to upload and download information using computer technology. The transfer of electronic

information is in fact a transfer of energy impulses strung together in particular streams or patterns.

"Just as the disciple enters the world of meaning and so he can interpret events, just as the Hierarchy works in the world of mediation, applying the Plan which the world of meaning has revealed, so the higher initiate works consciously in the world of purpose which the Plan implements, the world of meaning interprets, and the world of events expresses in sequential order and under the evolutionary Law."[61]

The Teachers ask of of those on the spiritual path to inquire into and reflect on certain questions regarding Recognition: "Why is it important to know about the existence of the Soul, the Hierarchy or the Plan?" "Do you recognize your own point in consciousness? "If you were deprived of such recognition, how would you feel right now?" "What would it be like to live through these times without recognition of the Plan or of its Planners (members of the Hierarchy), or of the reason why They are actively reaching out to humanity with the three recognitions?"

To the last question the following is given to stimulate further reflection on Their response which is as follows:

1. Penetrating through meditation or reflection into these Recognitions will bring calmness and stabilize the emotional body.
2. Recognition of the soul will serve as a lifeline during traumatic world events.
3. Through the insights of one's own soul, the mind is enlightened. Pearls of wisdom can be shared with others who may be searching for answers.

4. It can lead to a breakthrough in understanding that the troubling events in the world are serving a divine purpose.
5. The ability to grasp divine purpose can fuel the transformation of consciousness.

The Teachers ask of all the spiritual seekers, the intelligentsia and people of good will, to ask questions and formulate their own responses, and to share their discoveries and insights. This is a law that leads to the ultimate recognition and realization of Truth.

"The unexamined life is not worth living"
-Socrates

27. *LAW OF ANALOGY OR CORRESPONDENCE*

This law is gaining importance. The Teacher DK in the books of Alice A. Bailey explains it as the interpretive Law of the system, and explains God to man by stating: "All souls are identical with the Oversoul; The microcosm (man and his physical body) is analogous to the macrocosm (the Solar Logos and His body, the solar system) is the Macrocosm and Man is the Microcosm."

In light of this fundamental analogy, truths about the nature of the particular may be inferred from truths about the universal, and vice versa. Ralph Waldo Emerson says this: "That Unity, that Over-soul, within which every man's particular being is contained and made one with all other; that common heart."

That entity called the soul is an aspect of every form of life from an atom to a man, and to a Logos. The relationship between

---

[61] The Rays and the Initiations, Alice A. Bailey

souls and the Oversoul is the basis for the scientific belief in Brotherhood. Technically, brotherhood is not an ideal but a fact. As man is a microcosm in relation to a Planetary or Solar Logos, the human kingdom stands as a macrocosm is to the animal, vegetable and mineral kingdoms just as the God of our planet stands as a macrocosm is to all the kingdoms to which Earth is home.

Analogy or correspondence (synonymous terms, except for a subtle difference) are used by the Teachers to illustrate and illuminate certain points of the Ageless Wisdom. For example: the goal for the evolution of the atom is self-consciousness as exemplified in the human kingdom. The goal for the evolution of man is a level of group consciousness, as exemplified by a planetary Logos. The goal for the planetary Logos is God-consciousness as exemplified by the Solar Logos.

Plato says in his Republic, that without the light of the sun, the eyes can not see any object. Thus, Plato called the sun the source of goodness. He goes on to say that the soul is analogous to the sun. The soul is man's source of goodness, because its light illumines the mind. In order for the senses and mind to register spiritual realities, it needs the light of the soul to apperceive them. The Teacher Plato is illustrating, using Analogy, that the true nature of reality cannot be comprehended by the ordinary senses.

In analogy, when comparing one whole to another such as man to cosmos, it is important to understand that, as Aristotle said, "the whole is greater than the sum of its parts." When we first saw the earth from space, we perceived the masterpiece as a whole and it evoked a sense of wonder and awe. In analogy the whole supports the part

and vice versa. So, this law challenges the analytical mind and reductionist theory which reduces things to parts. This law encourages us to consider interconnectedness and wholeness in terms of the fundamental nature of reality.

The subtle difference mentioned earlier, is that in analogy there is similarity, but not in detail. In correspondence there is practically identical expression in detail, usually on a lower level.

A man, when occupied in creation of any kind, and in the process of producing forms on earth which embody an idea is functioning as a Logos. This is an example of analogy.

The senses and the etheric body of a human being serve as a perfect example of correspondence: The physical sense of hearing has its psychic correspondence in clairaudience. This leads eventually to mental telepathy and finally to a higher correspondence called intuition. Physical sight leads to clairvoyance. This leads eventually to spiritual vision and finally to the higher correspondence called identification. The sense of touch leads to sensitivity. This leads eventually to spiritual aspiration, to recognition and finally to spiritual impressibility. Another correspondence is the soul (as mentioned earlier) of a human being corresponding to the Sun. In a higher correspondence, the spirit of a human being corresponds to the great central sun of the galaxy.

This law works to bring the mind back into alignment with the soul. As the Law of Recognition states, the light of the soul, illumining the mind makes possible the recognition of subjective reality. As the personality becomes more familiar with the soul, the mind will eventually realize a deeper truth this law points to, which is, it is the truth of goodness that makes possible to soul's ability to know, which it bequeaths upon the receptive mind. Goodness or Good is right relation between all that exists and the Cause of existence. The Good is in essence, Love itself.

Metaphor and symbol are methods that work very well with this law, which the Teachers use quite often to guide, instruct and evoke response. As an example of metaphor being used to evoke response is the Teacher DK using the analogy of the sun. He has said in Alice A. Bailey's books, that the senses and thinking alone, are not enough to solve humanity's problems. There must be soul illumined thinking at this time, if humanity is to avert catastrophe and survive.

Some people think of Earth as a school for spiritual growth and this is true. But, many would be surprised to know that it goes deeper than that. It was not the original plan for the Earth to suffer to the degree that she has. The Planetary Logos long ago, volunteered for a great sacrifice, but the sacrifice was greater than had been anticipated. A call for help went out and many souls answered. Because of the great sacrifice of the Earth and the point in evolution reached, it was decreed that the Earth shall no longer be a school for discordant souls and a planet of pain and suffering.

Our blue planet is known throughout the universe for its sacrifice, an expression of the Law of Sacrifice and a window into how this law relates the part to the whole. It was divine goodness that impelled the Planetary Logos to ensoul the Earth, just as it is goodness that impels the soul to ensoul the form for the redemption of matter.

The workings of this law allows that which is normally unknowable, to become known to the individual who learns and knows how to use it. It is a wonderful tool for soul growth. Some use it consciously and deliberately, while others may not even be aware that they are using it. Used consciously, it will increase the clarity of vision and enable the mind to penetrate the hidden mysteries, and shed light on many a paradox.

Correspondence reveals the innate interconnectedness of all things in the universe and provides insight into their spiritual reality. For example, the concept of dark matter was known to the great Persian and Greek Initiates such as Zoroaster and Pythagoras, over 2,500 years ago. They discovered the correspondence of darkness to spirit, darkness, not in the negative sense of good and evil, but as the indefinable, indescribable nature of pure spirit that lies behind Light and Consciousness itself.

Dark matter cannot be seen, touched, smelled, or weighed. Dark matter does not absorb or reflect light and is therefore invisible. It is considered to be a non material substance and was first discovered by astro-scientists while doing research with the Hubble space telescope. Modern science is just now recognizing the existence of a dark matter that substands the physical universe But, science is yet to understand spiritually the correspondence of dark matter to spirit.

The correspondence of dark matter and spirit will remain a mystery to scientists until they understand it from the perspective of spirit. Then science will make the analogy and correspondence. The Black Hole at the center of the galaxy is the closest physical symbol of Spirit so far. Spirit holds the key for science in understanding the entire functioning of the universe.

Form corresponds to soul and soul corresponds to spirit. Personality contact with the soul corresponds to soul contact with the monad or spirit.

When the Ageless Wisdom refers to "darkness" as the one true actuality, the basis and root of light, without which the latter could never manifest itself, nor even exist"[62], it is trying to clarify an ageless wisdom concept so the mind can understand certain spiritual realities. In this case, it is the relationship between consciousness, light and spirit—darkness as pure Spirit, an absolute form of light beyond light.

As humanity's consciousness expands, these analogies will be transformed into living truths. Science will follow and understand why there is a correspondence between darkness and pure spirit. Light and Darkness is one of the most challenging of spiritual truths to convey using analogy, but pondering on analogy starts the mind thinking and has an expansive effect on consciousness.

The language of geometry is gaining recognition in the world once again as it did during the Renaissance. The philosopher, geometer Matila Ghyka in his book "The Geometry of Art and Life" quotes from his study of the phi proportion, found in nature and man: "You will know, as far as it is allowed to a mortal, that Nature is from all points of view similar to itself." The phi number, 1.618.....(never ending), R.A. Schwaller de Lubicz says it holds many secrets and is the number that lies at the heart of what the Egyptians call "the scission of unity", the genesis of creation. The

universe uses this number because its mathematical and proportions are the heart of this law. All Logos use the functional power of phi to relate the part and the whole, in the genesis of creation. One of the reasons, it is said that "God Geometrizes".

The correspondences or analogies that exist between the macrocosm and the microcosm has been summarized by Hermetic philosophy as: "As Above, So Below,". All parts of a design, from a work of art to the universe, when related to each other and to the whole through geometric harmony, will be found to express the aesthetics of unity and beauty. In this view, the human organism in its form, function and essence represents the organizing principles of the entire universe.

Analogical thinking was the foundation of the symbolic method of teaching in the ancient mystery schools. It must be borne in mind that no analogy is ever exact in detail but only in certain broad basic correspondences. Unchangeable points of similarity will always be found. In looking at creation, no two details are exactly alike but they are similar. This aspect allows for a practical understanding of the nature of those things that are beyond normal understanding.

By understanding the creative aspect of the Universal Mind, one can understand the creative aspect of the human mind. For example, the architecture of ancient temples based on the anatomy of the human being is essentially the cosmos in symbolic form.

The ancient master builders used the geometry that this law represents in their architectural masterpieces, some still standing today, though in silence, to teach their

---

[62] The Secret Doctrine, Vol I.

students the universal principles of spiritual development.

By understanding this law, one comes to understand universal processes. The Law of Correspondence or Analogy is considered a universal law because all material and spiritual manifestations in the universe are capable of analogy and correspondence.

This law does not recognize separation or the apparent separation in the divisions of polarities, gender, cause and effect, the part and the whole, the one and the many, but is the living spirit behind unity and beauty, and lives in the relationship of each microcosm to each macrocosm and each aspect of polarity.

As Helena Blavatsky says in the Secret Doctrine about this law: "It is the guiding law in Nature, the only true Ariadne's thread that can lead us, through the inextricable paths of her domain, toward her primal and final mysteries".

"As Above, So Below"
-The Emerald Tablets

28. LAW OF UNITY

The Law of Unity is that law which does not recognize separation. It ignores the appearance of separation in the apparent divisions of polarities, gender, cause and effect, the part and the whole, the one and the many. In this realization each is an integrated part of the whole. It is with this law that the evolutionary process is identified.

The law sees neither night nor day, but the night-day process; neither right nor wrong, but the right-wrong process; neither the pleasure nor the pain, but the pleasure-pain process; neither the one nor the all, but the oneness of the one life, whose cells and souls work together even in the appearance of division, recognizing such division, but emphasizing the unity of the parts.

The Law of Unity sees loss and gain, life and death as reality experiencing itself through the evolution of consciousness. Unity is the mode of reality experiencing itself. We are all connected, all carry the seed of divinity. This is the way we begin and the way we evolve into eternity.

It is only while in the third dimension of physical form because of the density of matter and the effect of its gravitational pull, on the higher self of the personality, that the experience of separation, an illusion in the thinking of a human being, occurs. To counteract this force or cancel its effects requires an equal and opposite force, that of soul consciousness.

As a result of this illusion, fear enters the emotional body because of this illusion and begins to eat away more deeply a human soul's connection to Source. But, as soul growth is experienced, in a small but profound way, all benefit from this law. Fear has a role and place in physical survival and safety, but as an emotion it does not lead to a positive sense of self or freedom. The choice is either to remain in fear or to evolve into fuller realizations of freedom based on the inherent divinity of the human soul.

It is this law that creates group unity and that consciousness uses to adapt form to life. Form follows consciousness and the soul is a unity of light and consciousness, colored by unique qualities. As mentioned in the previous law, the totality of all souls is the Over-soul. With its unique divine qualities, its attractive force is exerting a pull on all souls -

a cosmic force of evolution itself. A Logos is a representative of the Over-soul.

The human soul is the self-conscious aspect of the soul in the phenomenal appearance of a human being or physical incarnation. The group consciousness of the soul retains the human state of consciousness, but adds its unique qualities of vibration, to the human unit consciousness through progress on the spiritual path until the soul is fully unfolded through the personality, until a unity is achieved.

When the incarnated soul or personality is fully aware of its soul nature, then the soul-infused personality advances to those higher levels of consciousness that embody unity. The key to humanity's potential lies in the unfolding of the soul.

The soul is group consciousness-a combination of the qualities God-consciousness and self-consciousness, and therefore a human being is capable of expressing three points of appearance: God or Unity Consciousness, Soul or Group Consciousness and Personality or Self-Consciousness.

In working with the laws, specifically those of vibration and polarity, it must be recognized that in the evolution of consciousness, one is dealing with duality, and that the highest unity is achieved when the dual relationship is perfected, when the One Life is no longer a theory but has been demonstrated in the loving and intelligent application of truth.

The realization of unity is a matter of progressively shifting the focus of attention from one form to another, and thus, to a higher standpoint, gaining a fresh glimpse of a possible truth. Throughout human history, each age (and the present is no exception)

has believed its grasp of reality to be greater and closer to the truth than ever before possible. In our solar system, the highest attainable level of consciousness is that of Unity Consciousness as embodied by our Solar Logos.

Yet, there are Unities that are a mystery even to the Logos of a solar system. All is One, and all that appears to be separate will be reality to those who follow the path of separateness. To those who follow the path of spiritual transformation, the universe will be found to be one totality, and they shall recognize its Unity and understand separateness is an illusion. The Law of Unity is the law that governs the divine spirit within all souls.

The Law of Karma works with this law to bring those who stray from the Law of Unity back into balance through divine justice. Human beings can either choose to become victims or masters of these laws.

"The deeper the self-realization of a person, the more they influence the whole universe by their subtle spiritual vibrations, and the less they themselves are affected by the phenomenal flux." - Sri Yukteswar

29. LAW OF VIBRATION

The Law of Vibration is a subsidiary law under the major Law of Love which governs this cycle of our solar system's evolution. The life impulse of love (and wisdom) is providing a constant vibratory stimulation to our entire solar system. When our solar system is finished, it will re-evolute de novo. This is all part of the cycle of life that is governed by the Law of Periodicity.

Vibration is the basis of manifestation, beginning with the logos, word or creative power of deity—dual, yet non-dual from which sprang the cosmos. The cosmos is made up of two fundamental vibrations: spirit and matter, with a third principle: consciousness, which link the two, derived from the blending of spirit-the giver, and matter-the receiver.

Nothing stands still; everything moves; everything vibrates. It is the Law of Cycles, progress and constant motion. As Pythagoras is quoted as saying: "All life is vibration", but what does that mean? It means that vibration is the effect of deity in manifestation and everything in the universe functions at a particular rate of vibration.

Vibration produces a response in matter. A logos works in this way with matter so that it may be manipulated for the unfolding of the divine plan and perfecting of logoic purpose. Using the Law of correspondence, it is this same mode of operation that allows the soul to call together the atoms from which molecules, cells, organs and so on coalesce to form an integrated organism.

We can know things by their vibration and things can be stimulated by vibration. Where there is unity of vibration there is the fulfillment of divine law. "If thine eye be single, all is light", said the Christ, signifying the oneness in vibration of a unified self. The same idea applies to the ability of individuals and groups to work in harmonious relationship.

Where does vibration come from? Vibration comes from deity. The Law of Love and Vibration, works with the principle that alike attracts like—movement, and this movement provides the lessons for humanity in spiritual growth of discrimination in terms of choice and response to vibration.

What is it that vibrates? It is energy or life (life being used here as a synonymous term for energy), which vibrates at different rates, between the two poles, in order for there to be manifestation. At its highest vibration, matter is spirit, and at its lowest vibration, spirit is matter. Life is both spirit and matter, one and forever inseparable. Spirit and matter are different aspects of the One Divine Life. Vibration makes manifestation possible.

As mentioned, there is a third principle of divinity. When spirit and matter unite, the living light of consciousness flashes forth. All three are inseparable from one another. So, we have a single reality, but at the same time a coexisting duality - spirit and matter; and at the same time, a coexisting trinity, spirit, matter and the resultant interaction which is consciousness. The soul is a unit of this creative and vitalized consciousness, a blend of spirit and matter.

This law explains that the differences between manifestations of the One Life into spirit, matter and consciousness are largely due to the different rates in vibration. Atoms can vibrate at such high rate that they appear motionless to the physical eye. At the other end of the scale are things that vibrate so slowly that they also appear to be motionless or non-existent.

Zero-Point Energy (ZPE) lives at the zero level of vibration, even though that is difficult to comprehend and it is the primordial energy in our universe. ZPE corresponds to the silence of pure spirit.

What is unknown to the general public and the majority of the mainstream science is that there is a non-thermal inexhaustible energy field. It obeys a law beyond the Law of vibration. ZPE will be the future energy source in the coming era. This future law is connected with the mystery of electricity, mentioned in Law #18.

The vibration of fiery love can counteract the strongest opposition of fiery opposition. Fiery hatred is fought with the fiery aspiration of love. Love works to further evolution and when we work with love we work with the power of Spirit. Through the powerful vibration of an all-encompassing love for all beings, this love unfolds in its radiation the seen and the unseen, all the potential of the soul, the loved and all that needs loving. When a human being radiates such a vibration of love, it is magnified.

The Planetary Logos is entering a field of higher vibrations and undergoing a cosmic initiation, a process that is affecting the consciousness and forms of all the kingdoms that comprise its life. In light of this, participating in this upward evolutionary flow causing planetary change, is the highest form of service one can perform at this time, but it requires raising one's awareness to understand that spirit infuses all forms with love. This is called vibrational resonance.

How does one change the physical state of the world? The sages Plato and Lao Tzu knew this well when they said that whoever wishes to put the world right should begin with the reform of himself, the first step in the whole process of building a better world.

Forms respond to vibration. Forms follow consciousness. This is the key to building the new world of Aquarius. When this law is intelligently grasped, the mind of a human being will recognize the power of vibration, the means of self-transformation and arrive at true Self-Knowledge, for every thought, word and action has its vibration.

"Action, vibration is what I see, thoughts, sounds expressed in forms of words, forms of motion. O, man. My Laws have ben violated continuously. I look not upon you with sorrow or impatience, who have to live the mortal cycle of your own creations. Try, O Man to learn. Try, O Man to learn."
-Messages From the Golden Density, George W. Van Tassel

30. *LAW OF COHESION*

This is the law responsible for divine coherence and is a branch Law of the Law of Attraction. In addition to vibration, for anything to be born, there must be that which controls the gathering in of substance.

It is a law that demonstrates in a threefold manner in our our solar system and its seven levels of vibration:

1. The Astral, (right above the Physical and just below the Mental) the level of fluidity and feeling from the perspective of the personality. From the top down this is the sixth level. This law on the Astral, demonstrates as astral love in all its personality consciousness expressions.

2. The Buddhic, (right above the Mental and just below the Atmic, atmic being a level of universal mind or divine thought). The Buddhic is the level of the intuition that allows for conscious spiritual perception of truth. This law on the Buddhic, demonstrates as love-wisdom irradiating the soul and is the level upon which Fifth Kingdom exists. When Buddhic love demonstrates through the soul-infused personality, it is magnetic.

3. The Monadic, (right above the Atmic and just below the Logoic, the logoic being Over-soul unity). The Monadic is

the level of individualized spirit, inclusive awareness of and identification with the whole. It is the Law of Cohesion on this level. This law on the Monadic, demonstrates as Love, the source and the monads of Love, the result. This will be better understood as soul consciousness unfolds. The Christ and the Masters are examples of Monadic love, demonstrating though the personality, in which the soul and the monad have fused.

How this law demonstrates depends upon the consciousness of the individual and which of the even vibratory levels his or her consciousness is identified with.

On the emotional or astral plane, feeling energies flow through the personality consciousness of humanity, the Fourth Kingdom, to bring about certain conditions in one's life or the environment according to individual desire or that of a nation. This might be health, needed supplies, money, etc.

Through the purified personality, the astral plane is a calm reflector of the love and wisdom coming from the Buddhic plane. Through the purified personality, the mental plane is a vehicle for the consciousness of the soul.

On the Buddhic level, the combined energies of Divine Love and Will, flow into the the light of the soul or group consciousness for the purpose of revealing or expressing an aspect of the Plan as formulated by the spiritual Hierarchy.

At the Monadic level, divine energies flow into the Masters on this level from the highest or logoic level (a level connected to the source of creation and the level upon which a Logos exists) for the purpose of divine creation.

But, in each case, without a coalescing or attractive energy, thoughts, feelings or ideas, would not come into form. It is this law that is the cohering force of our solar system, which issued from the Word. When the Word ceases, vibration and coherence will cease. Then for the solar system, what is known as a "universal night" of rest will ensue, to be followed once again by a "universal day" of manifestation.

Cohesion is the hallmark of our solar system. The goal of our Solar Logos is for all of its parts to come together as one. It is the love-wisdom aspect of deity, which is the sounding note of our Solar Logos that brought our solar system into manifestation and under this law holds it together as a unit, just as the soul's note holds the atoms, molecules and cells together as one cohesive unit called the physical body.

In terms of spiritual group activity, cohesion is another term for mutual cooperation and harmonious relationship between members of the group and their activities. Cohesion promotes unity and harmonious cooperation, not disunity, repulsion or separation.

The major focal point of energy to be found in human beings is that of the soul, not the personality, and the potential of the soul lies in its potency as an agent of cohesion and of integration, and a greater potential yet to be expressed - that of demonstrating the quality of soul, just as the Solar Logos is seeking to demonstrate the divine quality of love-wisdom.

In the earlier stages of human evolution, it is the coherence aspect that is demonstrated. In the soul stages of human evolution it is the Law of Cohesion that demonstrates. Again, this will be better understood as soul consciousness unfolds.

In the new era, humanity can look forward to the the energy of divine love, working out through groups and the divine Plan. This is such a departure from perception as we know it on earth today that we will truly feel like new human beings endowed with the consciousness to perceive frequencies and vibrations of light, hitherto unknown and invisible. It is the Law of Cohesion that will make group work, magnetic and radiatory. "Group radiatory love" (see Ch. IV) is what the Masters Morya and KH call one of the eight of group activity when a group is functioning with soul consciousness and demonstrating group cohesion.

"There is no such thing as separation.
Morya loves my students,
as I [KH] do His"[63]

31. *LAW OF RHYTHM*

This is a law that deals with the health and development of the aspirant or disciple on the mental, emotional and physical levels. The training of aspirants and disciples in the new era will be cyclical and will have its ebb and flow like everything else in nature. Understanding the Law of Cycles brings knowledge of the evolutionary process and a realization of the rhythmic work of creation. Rhythm, ebb and flow, and the measured beat of the pulsating life are always the flow of the universe. In learning to respond to the vibration of high influences, rhythmic periodicity must be kept in mind.

Our Solar Logos, whose quality or basic motive is love-wisdom, seeks to demonstrate on a grand scale the great love aspect of divinity while adhering to the Law of

Rhythm. In this respect, the Law of Rhythm and its relationship with the spiritual quality of number needs mentioning.

Metaphysically, eleven is a number that symbolizes consciousness expansion and new beginning. Our sun's sunspot activity follows a nearly eleven year cycle of periodicity. Eleven, a double integer is a balanced feminine-masculine number, representing a new cycle of becoming and creative potential. The moon, associated with the feminine principle, follows a twenty eight day cycle. The moon, moving through the twelve constellation in its yearly rhythmic cycle and its 28 day monthly cycle, will be better understood in their significance to the growing, manifestation and building process, not just agriculture but to a works of art and architecture. In the new era of light, many fascinating and practical applications will come forth regarding this law.

The Solar Logos is seeking unity and rhythm in the relationship of its physical and spiritual nature. This great Being's evolutionary purpose is to have all parts of its solar life, physical and spiritual, vibrate in synchrony with its consciousness; to bring its manifested parts into rhythmic balanced interplay.

Rhythm is the highest vibratory expression of motion and that which vibrates rhythmically is of a very high frequency. The Solar Logos' rhythm is conditioning the lower rhythm of the solar system, just as the soul's rhythm is conditioning the lower rhythm of the persona. However, it is free will which can delay or assist the process. Adhering to the Law of love assists the process of rhythmic balanced interplay.

---

[63] 1994 - 1997, Letters

When the people of a planet live in harmony with the natural ebb and flow of life, they connect their collective rhythm with that of the planetary Logos. This creates a balanced flow of giving and re-giving between our planet, other resonant planets, and the heart beat of light and love emanating from the center of our galaxy. This increases the rhythmic balanced interplay our Solar Logos seeking to achieve.

There is one rhythm and that is the rhythm of the Creator of All. It is the rhythm of goodness. Divine rhythm enables one to see harmony in discord; order in apparent chaos. It is expressed in the statement: "It is the work of God and He does all things well." (Mark 7:31)

When human life is not aligned with this law, then regulation comes through Saturn, the cosmic disciplinarian and through Pluto, the destroyer of obstacles. The evolutionary flow of life observes this law, above all laws. The Teacher DK, in Discipleship in the New Age (vol.I) says that "love pulses through the universe in a divine rhythm".

Humanity is free not to conform to spiritual law, but Saturn brings in the consequences. The Plutonian force works more intensely than Saturnian force, through crises and conflicts to teach the wisdom of this law as required by stronger measures.

For example, without adapting to the Law of Rhythm, the cause of suffering continues as long as the soul remains under the lower rhythmic control of form. There is a natural tendency of form to hold on to material things and not know when to change or let go. What will it take for humanity to accept to the wisdom of God's laws?

On the physical plane, this principle is the most visible of all principles and its power is observed within the forces of nature that move the waves and tides of our oceans and the constant changes of the seasons. It is observed in the constant cycles of life, death, and the rebirth of all things, the rise and fall of governments and nations, the constant creation and destruction of suns, worlds, and galaxies.

Energetically, it is observed in the behavior of the electricity, light, and heat as they vibrate between higher and lower octaves. Rhythm on the mental plane is experienced as the wide mood swings that human nature displays. On the emotional plane it can be experienced as extreme happiness, and then swing to extreme sadness - from a gentle behavior to an extremely violent behavior in the blink of an eye. Rhythm is the Law of karmic compensation and maintains balance in all things.

The return swing of the pendulum is certain, and there is no escape from the effects of this immutable law. This law holds us true to what we believe, or disbelieve, and compensates us accordingly. Rhythm perpetuates the phenomenon of time. It is a teacher in the use of of thought, energy and time.

Either humanity uses the law to its evolutionary advantage, or the opposite. Universal Law is a door that swings in both directions. It swings according to where we chose to place our beliefs and whether or not our belief system allows us to see the truth as it really is.

If a person does not want to know or care, then such a person will evolve through the slow process of evolution. Nothing in the universe can, or is allowed to stand still. This law that is closely connected with the Law of Vibration makes certain of that.

The laws of vibration and rhythm can have a field day with a person who does not realize the effect the universal laws have.

All manifestation is the result of active energy producing certain results and expenditure of energy in any one direction will produce an equal expenditure in an opposite direction.

Synchronization of the laws of vibration and rhythm, says the Teacher DK, will occur as more of humanity enters the silence of the high places, those states through which pure love and wisdom flow.

The Law of Rhythm governs all evolutionary processes. It is this law that guides one of the eight qualities of group activity, that of group rhythm.

Alice Bailey in her book, Glamour, A World Problem said: "Humanity will find itself entering into the silent places where the Masters of the Wisdom dwell, and will work in group rhythm with Them, obeying thus the laws of the spiritual realm, which are the subjective laws of God." In the new era, humanity will be guided by the Masters of the spiritual Hierarchy, who embody the wisdom of this great law.

32. LAW OF LOVING UNDERSTANDING

This is the law for the next unfoldment of consciousness for the human kingdom as it shifts it identity from the personality to the soul, which will bring with it the right use of the mind. Soul unfoldment will bring the control over its vehicle of expression, the personality. Overdevelopment of the intellect with its sense of self has reached its limit, threatening the life of the planet.

Where there is a preoccupation with intellect in its analysis and comparison of parts, there is no room in the mind to register synthesis, intuitive impulses or loving understanding. These are all terms that the ancient sages, mentioned earlier, called the "intelligence of the heart". Loving Understanding is a spiritual quality of intelligence that is centered in love and unity. It is beyond comparison. When one has Loving Understanding, one has developed the functional consciousness of the soul.

Loving Understanding is the faculty of synthesis in the coordination of ideas. It was Schwaller de Lubicz, in his book, The Temple in Man, that first called "the intelligence of the heart", functional consciousness. Schwaller's background in hermeticism and alchemy, enabled him to read the Egyptian hieroglyphics architectural symbolism of the temples and with the support of his wife Isha, daughter Lucie and friends, made possible the sharing of the "intelligence of the heart" with the world, nearly eighty years ago.

There is an impulse toward synthesis, de Lubicz wrote, that manifests through the sympathetic nervous system and has a direct physical reaction upon the heart. In the new era, it will be the process of initiation, scientifically applied to the expansion of consciousness, within the new temples of initiation that will demonstrate the efficacy and beauty of de Lubicz's discovery that man is a living temple of synthesis. Along with the externalization of the Masters, humanity will create a sustainable golden culture based on loving understanding.

De Lubicz's wrote: "Intelligence is the intelligence of a human being, who incarnating all the possibilities of the Universe, knows this universe without having to reason it." It is this law that is behind the realization that essential unity equally preserves essential diversity.

However, it should be clear that the intelligence of comparison and analysis is a necessary stage in the evolution of constitutes the psychological consciousness. Mind distinguishes human beings from the animals. The "good news" is that the soul of humanity is awakening, and realizing that intellect and science alone are not enough to solve the problems of humanity.

Humanity is at a crossroads and must choose to either take the path spiritual transformation or stay on the path it is on which threatens all life on earth. This is a law that supports an "intelligence of the heart" morality, which says that each person is bound to all, each is responsible for, and benefits from, the good and evil deeds of all.

A sense of the urgency for change is now emerging and embryonic seeds of loving understanding are developing in parts of humanity, but a critical mass in consciousness is needed if humanity is to be ready for the shift to the New World. The pituitary and pineal bodies of the brain respond to the vibration of love. Selfless service and self-transformation also helps to activate the pineal and pituitary glands. So to does taking responsibility for one's actions and the welfare of the planet.

When a human soul is dedicated to the life of all humanity, the qualities of Loving Understanding flows more freely into human consciousness. This allows for the dormancy of pineal and pituitary bodies, to once again awaken. These two glands within the head, when fully activated, are responsible for awakening the intelligence of the heart.

The light of the soul can dissolve and transmute the crystallization of these two glands which has resulted from attachments to the form side of life. Such attachments may be ideals that no longer serve a soul purpose. In this way, the process of self-transformation as a spiritual practice can scientifically be applied in practical ways. The pineal body, also called by Plato the "eye of the soul" is most responsive to the light of the soul.

This law holds the key to creating that space in one's mind of freedom, for new ideas and ways of creative living to flow into one's life and consciousness. The new age of the soul is about life and consciousness first, and secondly, the form.

In the New World, evolving towards a greater understanding of love and wisdom will be paramount as humanity sees that growth in consciousness is linked to the soul. There is a growing understanding that the human being is a spiritual being, a soul that exists on a higher vibratory level of existence, temporarily incarnated in form for extended learning. A human being does not have a soul; a human being is the soul.

This is a law for which present day language is inadequate to express its full functional effects on consciousness. The Teacher DK says in the book Esoteric Psychology I by Alice Bailey that: "The Law of Loving Understanding is a quite inadequate and sentimental phrase for a scientific expression of a great coming evolutionary development in the human consciousness. But, until that development is an accomplished fact, we have no means whereby to express the true significance of the underlying idea."

The realization of the Teacher's words will lead to the recognition of God or divinity as undeniable truth, to the recognition of humanity as an expression of the divine, and the fact of humanity as a whole, not a part of a planetary life, but identified with the wholeness of planetary life. It will be the group consciousness of individuals and spiritual groups in the new era, who will demonstrate the qualities of loving understanding.

It is truly joyous to know that after a long separation (only in human minds) from the loving Master of Wisdom, that this veils which separates our two realms will soon be lifted. Once again, as in Atlantis, humanity and the Hierarchy will walk together on this beloved plant but this time in Loving Understanding, with a sense of responsibility and an unshakeable love.

A more mature humanity will work with clear vision, free from glamours of various kinds, paving the way for new experiences in the evolution of consciousness. The more consciously humanity is aligned with this law, the more the dynamics of unity will manifest on Earth. Loving Understanding is a functional quality of consciousness, and humanity is demonstrating its willingness to be impressed by it, as evidenced by the growing number of human beings who make up the people of goodwill and groups of spiritual service, willing to take responsibility in transforming the world.

Loving Understanding is a principle of life that will transform consciousness through right relationship and synthesis, words that will become clearer as soul consciousness unfolds. The overall purpose of this law is to bring ideas and impulses from the divine realms into the awareness of the human consciousness. For now, the Teacher DK can find no better words to adequately express its highly scientific nature

and functional effects than the words: Loving Understanding.

33. *LAW OF ASSEMBLY*

This is a law with a rather unusual name. It governs those great procedures which are responsible for the bringing in of extraplanetary energies for the redemption of worlds which is carried forward by that great life —a planetary Logos. It is a Law of high order, which at present operates only in the Council Chamber of Shamballa and unless one is a member of the Spiritual Hierarchy, the process is beyond the capacity of the human mind to comprehend. It is a law that will be synchronized with the Law of Loving Understanding.

The Teacher DK explains that in Shamballa, there is awareness of the whole of the solar system, where the divine consciousness of Will operates. It is the highest vibratory level of earth seven levels of existence. It is a focal point of synthesis, for energies that are assembled and brought together by the planetary Logos and an assembly of divine coworkers, in order to create a manifestation adequate to His unfolding purpose.

Within the confines of Shamballa, this requires a process of highly evolved wills of love, wisdom and synthesis, that are capable of eliminating and substituting courses of action and energies, so that the Earth system steadily evolves into greater expressions of wholeness.

This process of assembly with its elimination and substitution, takes place with a great deal of peacefully directed will, at the beginning and end of an age. A lower correspondence of this activity are the egalitarian assemblies and intergovernmental organizations of the world that meet and operate to maintain international peace and security through promoting a common will and dialogue around the common good.

This is the law that is impressing itself upon those receptive minds in fields of government, leadership, economics, science, health, human rights, the sharing of resources, international law, education, etc.

Each solar age of approximately two thousand years, dictates the course of action for the planetary Logos and the Law of Assembly governs the process. It is closely related to the highest form of cosmic fire: Electricity. It deals with the processes which inform the formulation of the plan by the spiritual Hierarchy, Who step down the electric fire of will down to the solar fire of love, and which the Christ then transmits into human consciousness. Where there are prepared minds or a welcoming vibration, there is greater success of impression.

The work of Shamballa is both cosmic and planetary in nature. Sanat Kumara and His coworkers are able to penetrate into extraplanetary spheres, and then focus or gather these energies for redemptive purposes. These focused or gathered energies influence the work of the spiritual Hierarchy, who are tasked with stepping down the energies thus gathered in Shamballa with love and wisdom, so that the plan can be useful and practical for humanity.

Through a corresponding process at a lower level, new systems of thought that better serve the common good slowly replace those that have served their evolutionary purpose. There must be receptive minds and hearts within humanity that can register the flow of spiritual ideas emanating from the spiritual Hierarchy for the upliftment of humanity.

The Law of assembly guides the spiritual sciences of Light and Energy utilized in the redemptive work of those who labor in the higher, subtler spheres of planetary and solar life. The assemblage of new and more correct approaches are alway replacing the old. This is an ongoing process. Christ's words about new wine and old wineskins, (Mark 2;22) alludes to this law which adapts form to consciousness.

More will be revealed about the Law of Assembly in the new era as human cooperation with the inner government of the planet unfolds. A preview of it has been presented so that those of a spiritual orientation can begin to grasp the scope, depth, and scale of this law and those who wield it.

"The building here to be carried forward, I would remind you, is not the building which is distinctive of the second divine aspect—that of Love-Wisdom. It is strictly connected with that of the first aspect of Purpose, Power or Will; it deals with the processes which precede the actual creative building, the drawing up of the blueprints (if I may use such a term) "within the confines of Shamballa," where high spiritual Beings must lay Their plans. This is a different process to the creative building process, and is related to a mysterious undertaking which is carried forward under the "Law of Assembly." -The Teacher DK, Discipleship in thee New Age (vol.II)

III
LAWS OF SOUL LIFE

The laws of soul life are seven in number and were first codified by the Teacher DK working with His amanuensis Alice A. Bailey, nearly eighty five years ago. They were given for the purpose of preparing awakening souls for group work to help further the plan. As the books of Alice A. Bailey are about the influence the soul will have on humanity, the laws of soul life are more specific.

DK in Alice A. Baileys book, A Treatise of White Magic, prefaces the laws of soul life by stating that "As love-wisdom through the medium of the heart center awakens, it leads to expansions of consciousness which initiates a man into his group life. He loses the sense of separateness, and finally emerges into the full light of realization—a realization of unity with his own indwelling God, with all humanity, with all souls in all forms of nature, and so with the Oversoul."

The sentient being known as man is a human soul with a physical body. The physical body partakes of decay and death, the rhythm of dense matter. However, the soul, the higher self of a human being is immortal. Due to its non-physical nature, it partakes of the rhythm of life and not the seeds of decay or death. The Teacher DK has said in the book by A.A.B., Esoteric Healing "In the future the Laws of soul life will negate or offset the laws of nature as the consciousness of the humanity evolves."

The nature of the soul is light and love. The consciousness of humanity cannot evolve without the soul.   The soul's nature is to grow the intensity of its light and love. The soul incarnates to evolve for the purpose

of gaining light to fulfill the potential of the divine spark at its core. The recognition of the soul and the essential truth about the soul are now emerging, through the intensifying changes a this time. This recognition is taking root within the consciousness of humanity, making humanity cognizant also of the Kingdom of Souls and a progressive Plan.

When the Teacher DK first introduced the Laws of Soul Life through the books of Alice A. Bailey, He put forth the question: "What is the overarching purpose of the soul laws? ", and the answer: "The Laws of Soul Life are laws concerned primarily with the establishing of the great Fellowship of the Universe. The laws of soul Life concern the life of the soul upon its own plane, and the relation which the blending soul and personality learn to establish with other souls and with the Hierarchy. These specific laws are not about the relation of soul to form but inter-soul relationship—group life, and with the synthesis underlying the forms."

Our planetary Logos, the divine Being that ensouls the Earth, is undergoing an expansion of consciousness. On the human level, this is corresponding to what is taking place in consciousness—a crisis of identification. Are we willing to shift our identification from that of the personality to that of the soul? If our answer is yes, and we do the work of self-transformation, as each is able, the Plan is being well served and will move forward.

"The scent of a Rose carries the purest vibration in olfactory. The Lotus blossoms into beauty amidst muck and mire. Sit long with

patience and observe. For this is the key to the unfoldment of the Soul."[64]

34. LAW OF SACRIFICE

This is the first of the seven Laws of Soul Life and it is a dominant world law that has been seriously misinterpreted by religions. It does not deal with sacrifice as the offering of material possessions or animals or human life to a deity as an act or means of salvation or atonement. It is not the means to salvation, but the urge, the divine impulse to salvation. It is concerned with giving and is related to group love, group understanding, group relations and group conduct.

It governs the appearing and the disappearing of universes, of solar systems, of races and of nations, of world leaders and world rulers, of incarnating human beings and of revealing Sons of God. It is the expression of a divine impulse, that of Giving.

The whole secret of the doctrines of "the forgiveness of sins" and of the "atonement" is hidden in one simple word: giving. It is the basis of the Christian doctrine of love and sacrifice. It is also the human instinct towards that which lies beyond dualities, the stage of essential oneness—"at-onement". Hence the emphasis laid, in the Piscean Age and under the influence of Christianity, on two qualities of the human spirit — forgiveness (note the word 'give' in forgiveness) and the capacity for spiritual self-transformation.

The idea that a single people benefit from sacrifice and death of a great Son of God, prophet or messiah, and enter a state of bliss in heaven by the merits of that substitutionary death, simply because of an emotional choice, ignoring millions of those who have made no such choice, nor had the opportunity to do so, is a distorted misrepresentation of the truth.

Giving is not to be confused with surrender. We are not speaking of surrender in the military sense of surrender or submission due to conflict or hostility. We are speaking of a spiritual surrender, a transfer of control from the personality to the expanded consciousness of the soul, so that life is lived as a soul—a willingness to give control over the soul.

When life is lived from that place, the struggle ceases because of an inner knowing and peace that things will always unfold in the right direction. When surrender is to a higher principle or energy such as the Will of God for the purpose of leading humanity into "fields" of peace, surrender becomes giving.

When group consciousness or the soul nature is carefully studied, the meaning of giving and surrender will take its rightful place in the human consciousness, and this law with all that it entails will be properly understood and applied. When the Law of Sacrifice is properly understood, the other laws will also be properly understood.

The manifestation of any form through the sacrifice or giving of some great life for the advancement of other evolving lives, that they may progress, is one of the fundamental methods of evolution in our universe.

Was it the divine instinct of love that created the worlds? One cannot know God's cosmic Intent until one has taken some of the higher initiations. But, we do know that for a Cosmic Life to appear or manifest in

---

the form of a universe, solar system or planet, there must be a will, a desire and an impulse to do so. When the cosmic creative act took place, the Cosmic Christ, (God as Love, the Son) was crucified on the cross of matter and by that great sacrifice, opportunity was offered to all evolving life in all kingdoms of nature and in all created worlds. Perhaps, creation is the supreme act of love, the great sacrifice.

On a corresponding level, the Christ's crucifixion 2000 years ago, created the opportunity for all humanity to progress. Christ's life demonstrated the necessity of sacrifice for spiritual awakening. The World Savior's triumph over death, gave humanity proof of the soul's immortality. Christ did not intend for man to focus on the act of the crucifixion as obeying 'the Will of the Father,' but rather on spiritual regeneration through self-transformation.

Christ's message 2,000 years ago, was to illustrate the nature of salvation by demonstrating the requirements for the path of return to union with the Divine: spiritual love, forgiveness and at-onement. The path of return begins in the heart. There can be no spiritual progress without a heart that is receptive to the down-pouring love of the Spirit.

There is a logical reason for this. Love is needed when it comes to learning about higher truth. Without love, learning about higher truth would be difficult. People would recoil from truths, such as the Law of Cause and Effect without the protective mantle of love and compassion for one's self and all living beings. Christ, who embodied the love of God, radiated a universal force that awakened people—that love creates the space for understanding karma and its transformation. All karma is a test of love.

When Jesus drank the cup and chose, it was to fulfill the law and Hid part of the Plan. His sacrifice was out of love for humanity, showing the way back to the Father. In the new era, when He returns to outer manifestation, to His all-encompassing love will be added Will, and those who accompany Him will lead humanity in the understanding of the Will, the Divine Laws, the Plan and the necessary adjustments to live as souls in a new world of etheric beauty and light.

Spiritual (not physical) crucifixion is a basic premise of all group work. It will be understood as the governing principle that causes each human unit to move from self-consciousness to group consciousness and finally to become a world server and re-give the gifts received of spiritual love, peace, and wisdom to others. Such is the workings of this law. The spiritual Hierarchy will show that there is nothing in life to fear, only to understand.

We owe all of our progress to the great Law of Sacrifice. It is also known as the "Law of those who choose to die." Not death as humanity understands it, but those who choose to give their lives freely and unconditionally to other souls and other life forms in other kingdoms so that they too may evolve.

The Teachers ask us to ponder and reflect: "What is the purpose of life?"

It will be realized that the baser instincts, particularly those that result in conflict and war, have their roots in fear, not understanding. The primal fear of man is physical death, or the extinction of the sense of self. In the new era, the truth will be revealed that death as humanity understands it, does not exist; it is a part of the path of return, as a doorway to a more subtler world where the light of truth illuminates all things in the light of love.

In the new era, the power of spiritual love will also remove a second category of human fear: that of abandonment, betrayal, and isolation. The pain of separation has been the breeding ground for anger and violence since the origins of the human species.

This spirit of sacrifice is always found when the spirit of Love is properly contacted, even in the smallest degree. The underlying impulse behind the loving will of God, or the will-to-love, is felt and understood, accompanied as this always is, by the desire to participate with others in a joyful spirit. A Great Unity or Life) comes into manifestation to give of Itself, so that the lesser lives and forms of existence are equally able to advance to the higher places of spiritual expression.

The giving of the greater for the lesser is the theme of the entire creative process and is the basic meaning of the phrase, "God is Love." There is a symbol to this law given by the Teacher DK in A Treatise on Cosmic Fire. It is a rosy cross with a golden bird hovering above it. The energy is the outpouring energy of harmony through conflict, a unifying harmonizing universal factor and also the reason why sacrifice is blended with pain and sorrow.

DK also makes the point known that the spiritual laws of our solar system have their planetary and celestial administrators. The Lord of Jupiter is responsible for giving the Law and the Lord of Saturn enables its manifestation, while the great Lord of Libra is the sponsor of the law. This demonstrates how the universal brotherhood work together under Law of sacrifice.

This law has a reciprocal nature to it which has led to the recognition of the soul in humanity. The sacrifice of the lower lives to release the saving energy of the higher, and at the same time the sacrifice of the higher lives to uplift the lower.

A clue to the spiritual unfoldment of humanity lies in reciprocal approach. It means that humanity must reach up as the Hierarchy reaches down. This creates a steadier flow of love and creates an evocative potency. The Teachers always ask us to remember, that with every step humanity takes closer to Them, They take many more steps closer to us.

The sacrificial instinct that has driven humanity forward, from its wild struggle for material well-being to the effort to ameliorate conditions, to the renunciation of gain for self and the performance of unselfish acts, are all expressions of divine love and a sacrificial heart, which are expressions of a still greater force in the creative process, that of the Divine Will.

This is a law that embodies the great lessons of every human soul on the spiritual path. At a point on the spiritual path, it represents a willingness to sacrifice all personality desires in support of Divine Will as perceived by the soul.

The Law of Sacrifice is what guides that quality of service in which there is selfless action for the greater good. If there is not a reciprocal approach on the part of humanity, that is, if humanity just sits around and waits to be saved by some supernatural means, it only delays humanity's spiritual unfoldment and the Plan, which includes the externalization of the Christ and the spiritual Hierarchy.

Humanity has a responsibility in the advancement of planetary evolution. A question to ponder is: What does reciprocal approach mean to you in terms of sacrifice?

True sacrifice infuses service with the spirit of life and is a blessing that flows into the world from a realized sense of Divine Will as the Will-to-Good, and an understanding of this law.

"Oh Man, Help Me to express the Oneness of each of us, That I may center all My parts in unity of Me and thee in harmony and Love, that none shall know the pain and sorrow, the heartbreak you did express yourself. I gave you Light of Life that you might extend My Action, and that others might feel the Joy of Me...that are in darkness bent; who are troubled-blinded and cannot see that I Am there. Extend the progress I have brought into being by lifting up another that I may feel the two-fold expression in grateful thanks."
-Messages from The Golden Density, George Van Tassel

35. *LAW OF MAGNETIC IMPULSE OR POLAR UNION*

This is the second of the seven Laws of Soul Life. Also known as the first step to spiritual marriage, or the Law of Polar Union. It deals with the primary realizations by any unit of consciousness, be it an atom or a human being, of its surrounding contacts or groups. It is a sensitivity born out of affinity by that unit which eventually leads to a relationship between the unit and its contacts or group.

It results in an eventual union between the part and the group, creating harmonious group relations. The symbol for this law is two fiery spheres united by a triangle of fire, representing balanced fiery aspiration (not unbalanced passion) in the interplay between souls (not personalities). This has the effect of creating a corresponding magnetic relationship of certain centers in the etheric body.

Through a proper understanding of this law, a person comes to a knowledge and realization of the subjective life of the soul and is better equipped to work in coordination with others, in and with form.

Living in the New Earth of etheric-physical substance will make subjective soul interaction more accessible. As soul interaction becomes more readily established, the Law of Attraction and the laws of soul life will be the main orchestrators of individuals and groups. These are groups for the purpose of establishing highly refined and ordered units of group activity, large and small, that will cooperate with the spiritual Hierarchy in carrying out the Plan.

By a correct understanding of this law, a disciple works consciously in form while remaining polarized in consciousness to the subjective levels of the soul. This is not the same thing as making sense contacts, for the relationship established is between higher selves and not between lower selves or personalities.

It is a spiritual union of a subjective nature on the level of group consciousness. It is not an individual's union with the inner christ or soul, which is continually unfolding within members of the group. It is an experience of subjective group unity.

This law concerns those inner subjective activities which are not primarily concerned with form life, but with soul life functioning behind the scenes, such as group cohesion, unity of purpose, group rhythm, etc. It is the law that governs the subtler relationships, interplays, and inter connections between groups of souls on the inner level, not the outer or form level.

The outward or visible unity of a group results from its ability to respond, via the growing consciousness of the soul, to the subtle magnetic impulses of a Master's ashram. Therefore, the need to meet as individuals, is not felt as a necessity by the members of the group, except under certain circumstances. The work goes on joyfully and efficiently, and when the individuals do feel a need to meet as individuals, higher wisdom guides the way.

At the level of the soul, there is no "my soul and your soul", there is only that sense of being part of a greater whole. In its broadest sense, this law concerns the interrelationship of all human souls within the life of what is called the Kingdom of liberated or enlightened Souls—the spiritual Hierarchy of the planet or the Fifth Kingdom. When a group feels a sense of unity with the inner ashram of the Master, it marks an achievement in group cohesion.

Closely related to the Law of Attraction or love, this law operates in the realm of the soul, the world of meaning rather than the world of phenomena or effect. Just as the Law of Attraction brings together men and women in a group effort, so the Law of Magnetic Impulse begins to control when the group unites to constitute themselves as a channel for Light, Love and the Will-to-Good.

This law governs the interplay between groups of souls in form and out of form. Just as purification, meditation and service have given an individual the ability to make soul contact, so groups of souls, through this law, will be able to make contact with higher sources of spiritual supply - great lives and forces of light. This law extends through the great chain of Hierarchy into the farthest reaches of the universe.

Recent observations by astronomers who have observed the merging of galaxies, and predicted in the far distant future that our galaxy will merge with the Andromeda galaxy, may be an analogy for this law on cosmic levels of form and consciousness.

Through the mastery of this law, higher available energies can be used for the working out of the Plan and Logoic Purpose. The Law of Magnetic Impulse is more than an alignment with a Master's group or right relationship with one's fellow group members. It is a relationship of a far greater and more vital thing because it is an achieved union between two kingdoms.

The term 'polar union' means a fusion between two groups, that of the outer or Fourth Kingdom and that of the inner or Fifth Kingdom, so that far higher forces of light can be channeled into the world.

As soul infused group work becomes more widespread and its activity more orderly, this law will come into greater activity and a greater understanding will unfold of the role of the human kingdom as a mediator between the higher spiritual realms and the three subhuman kingdoms.

The symbol for the Law of Polar Union is also the originator of the sign for Libra. Libra represents balance and service. Because of the large role that humanity has to play in the Divine Plan of God, this law will be a determining factor. However, this will not be the case until the majority of human beings learn what it means to be a mediator—act as a transmitters of light, energy and spiritual potency to the subhuman kingdoms.

The aggregated aspiration and dedication of the group under this law, makes possible what would not be possible alone—an intensity of realization. Since the Teacher DK opened the spiritual opportunity in the Wesak, to the western world in 1939, many groups have realized the importance of polar union, of working together in unity with the spiritual Hierarchy.

It is important to understand about this law, that there is no personal ambition implied and no personal union sought. This is not the mystical union of the past or of mystical traditions. As mentioned, it is not the alignment and union with a Master's group or the fusion with one's inner band of pledged disciples, or even with one's own soul. All of these are preliminary implications and of individual application.

It is worth repeating that this union is a far greater and more vital thing because it is a union of kingdoms and it manifests the energy of love and wisdom, that which our Solar Logos is trying to achieve. This Law of soul life is the subjective aspect of the Law of Love as it operates in the realm of souls.

36. *LAW OF SERVICE*

This is the third of the seven Laws of Soul Life. The Law of Service grows naturally out of the successful application of the Science of the Antahkarana and the Science of Meditation, both under the coming Science of Light of the new era. It will be the Law of soul activity and in the new era, humanity will come to understand this law as a science and as an extension of what Christ expressed two thousand years ago: "For even the Son of Man came not to be served but to serve others and to give his life as a ransom for many." (Mark 10:45)

All those who are being prepared for initiation will at some point be faced with drinking the "chalice", the symbolic the cup of service. This law holds within itself the mystery of divine destiny. The meaning of

Christ's words when He drank of the cup, and said "Not my will but Thine"(Luke 22:42), was not a statement of acceptance of pain and of an unpleasant future or of death, as commonly understood by the orthodox.

It was the will of His soul to make contact with the will of the Divine in Shamballa and in so doing, established a relationship, a frail line of connecting energy, yes, but real nonetheless.

For those who are beginning to live consciously as souls, who are committed to serve humanity, the divine plan and the spiritual Hierarchy at this time, there is a message the Masters wish to convey on Christ's behalf: "To ignite the inner fires of all who can be reached with this essential message: A new Earth is being born. Those who can hear, will be its pioneers. Those who can see, will know the truth of My words, for this new world will draw the heart of humanity into visible manifestation by the glow of its love. Do not fear but rejoice in what will be coming forth into the light of day. Prepare to be blinded by this light and astonished by its power to heal the human heart." [65]

Only when love finds its outlet in service can a human being begin to measure up to its innate but unexpressed spiritual potential. This law is connected with the Law of Hierarchy where each act of selfless service strengthens the forces of light and humanity's connection with the higher spiritual realms. This produces a corresponding activity in the personal life, an activity which the Masters call, Service. Herein lies growth through service.

The Teacher DK in Education in the New Age by A.A.B., says that "Service is the true

---

[65] The Coming One, thecomingone.org

science of creation and is a scientific method of establishing continuity". A term the Masters use for this law is the Law of Water and of Fishes, water representing "life more abundant", so that men and women, representing the fishes, could partake of the needed living waters of the Spirit.

The symbol of this law is a pitcher on the head of a water-bearer standing in the form of a cross. The zodiac constellation of Aquarius is depicted with a pitcher of water on the shoulders of a water-bearer signifying service, while the water bearer stands perfectly balanced, indicating balance, poise and stability. As long as one is a balanced and stable vehicle for the life of spirit to flow through and into the world, service will demonstrate with a beauty and perfection unique to the situation.

These three sciences:

1. Science of Meditation
2. Science of the Antahkarana
3. Science of Service

will be integral to the educational process in the new age. They form a triangle of balanced energy. Skill and proficiency in these sciences will a part of group training and education in the new era.

The Law of Service, which governs the science of service, will foster the illumining of the mind, the needs of the group and the goal of world service, replacing self-interest, personal ambition and emotional idealism. The energy of this law expresses as a steady and balanced commitment, not as passionate devotion or unrealistic idealism, through a the personality that is becoming soul-infused. It produces intelligent service guided by the light of love.

It must be born in mind that the pledge of a group member who works within a Master's group has a cautionary note attached to it. After the pledge is administered, if the shirking of responsibility is a conscious action, there are karmic consequences for both the group member and the Master. To be in a group connected with a Master requires sacrifice of time and personal interest, self-effort, will and the ability to work without attachment and without interfering with the individual rights of others.

When service is rendered with a pure heart, the living soul force pervades the service. Service is not something to be forced. It needs to flow freely as impersonal love that spontaneously springs into action as a result of sensitivity to the need.

The Teacher DK defines service as the spontaneous effect of soul contact. True spiritual service is not a method of saving the world but a demonstration of the life of the soul.

The soul's natural tendency is to serve a higher will, and it is this quality of the soul that produces the sense of responsibility in the personality, Contact with the soul, naturally leads to service in the outer world. Service therefore cannot be taught. It is the natural result of soul contact. It is the result of contact with the inner sun of love.

The service of a loving heart has a transforming effect on the entire personality. So says the Teacher DK in Esoteric Psychology: "Service is not simply an activity of some person or group doing something with good intention for another person or group. Service is the result of a tremendous inner happening, and when that result is brought about, it will be found to have produce changes in the lower consciousness, a tendency to turn away from the things of the personal self to the larger issues of the group, a reorientation which is real and expressive and a power to change conditions which is the demonstration of something dynamically new. Thus the true server comes into possession of his instruments for service, and thenceforth creative work in accordance with the Plan can go forward."

There is a divine limitation associated with this law. DK (also in Esoteric Psychology by A.A.B.) says: "God, in His wisdom chose to limit Himself so that the work of evolution proceeds solely through the medium of self-chosen builders and under the direction of those men and women whose lives are being transformed through soul contact and creative service, and who constitute the planetary Hierarchy. These are the factors which govern souls on their plane, condition their activity, and, within the limits wherein they work, are the factors which (in time and space) condition and limit Deity, for such is His divine Will." For God to place a limitation upon Him/Herself and not interfere in the evolutionary work of planetary Hierarchies explains an interesting aspect about divine will and its relation to free will and service.

There will be many avenues and opportunities for service in the new era. The Teacher DK has this key message to share about the Law of Service from Esoteric Psychology: "In this work many can have a part. The Law of Service has been thus outlined in an endeavor to make one of the most esoteric influences in the solar system somewhat clearer in our minds. I call you to service, but would remind you that the service discussed here will only be possible when we have a clearer vision of the goal of meditation, and learn to preserve, during the day, the attitude of inner spiritual orientation. As we learn to detach in our consciousness from ourselves as the central figure in our life drama, then and then only can we measure up to our real potentialities as servers of the Plan."

37. *LAW OF REPULSE*

This is the fourth of the seven laws of soul life. This is also known as the Law of All Destroying Angels, and its symbol is an angel with a flaming sword that turns in all directions. It is the angel who guards the treasure and drives man out in search of another way in, forcing him through the cycle of rebirth until he finds the way, through spiritual growth. Angels know that the treasure of eternal life must be carefully guarded, for it is not easily attained. It is a Law of activity and soul stimulation.

The energy of this law is a repulsive energy (not of aversion, but repelling), a dispersing factor. It functions to stimulate and inspire the seeker by demonstrating the power of love and wisdom as an aspect of the will of the soul, using spiritual love to repulse that which is undesirable to the higher self, the true man/woman. It rejects, until that which the heart desires is found. The why and how of this law may seem mysterious, but it emphasizes the value of obstacles on the path of ascent.

The depictions of Jesus with a fiery heart, can be interpreted in light of this law. In the Gospel of Thomas Jesus says: "He who nears to me nears the heart of the fire." Sacred fire is a power of divinity and it generates a field of love and wisdom, that alchemizes away the impediments of the ego, so the fundamental nature of the soul can shine through, once the inner divinity within us is acknowledged.

In Hindu cosmology this sacred fire is called Agni and is seen as a transformative force, purifying, illuminating, and as Divine Presence representing life and energy. In the New Era this divine fire called Agni will assume due importance in human life.

Unless there is a thread of light in our consciousness to act as a channel for some soul contact, some measure of soul force, the activity of this law will not be registered and what this law can convey to the intelligence will remain unknown, unrealized and useless. The full power is felt when the the personality is made a pure vehicle for the soul.

When a person enters the spiritual path and progresses, this law begins to function in his or her life, unconsciously at first. The mind comes to appreciate and understand the nature of the path, the nature of the ego or personality in relation to the soul or higher self and that this involves the development of discernment between illusion and reality, and the ned for purification.

Treading the spiritual path of transformation, the same path trodden by Buddha, Christ and all the Masters, involves the activity of this law. It stimulates detachment, determination and acceptance. With each step on the path, if trodden with pure motive, the spiritual seeker comes closer to achieving freedom from the illusion of separation.

It must be born in mind that attachment to any form, even if it is a teaching or a Master, is an obstacle to the realization of this law. The nature of the soul is love, light and the will to serve the Plan. It is not obedience to Masters, but obedience to the

divine principle of the Light of the ALL in All. This one concept of repulsion (not exclusion) brings the understanding that the progress of brotherhood is not possible without the activity of this law and power of the soul to ignite the fire of universal brotherhood in others.

In the words of one of the Teachers: "The community, being a fellowship first of all, sets as a condition for entrance two conscious decisions: labor without limit and acceptance of tasks without rejection."[66] If there is love and the will to continue on the path, the power of love to repel (not exclude) and transform will be operative in our lives. Support will be provided by the soul and higher realms, and with it the power to work (not struggle) without limit, accepting the tasks that come with it.

38. *LAW OF ELEVATION OR GROUP PROGRESS*

This is the fifth of the seven laws of soul life. This law begins to function and register in the personal consciousness when the members of the the group achieve certain definite realizations, and knows certain ideals as facts in experience such as non-sentimental, consciously embraced brotherhood, and harmlessness and discrimination between the real and the unreal. It also includes trust in the guidance and wisdom of the Fifth Kingdom. This is vital for the progress of the group.

The symbol for this law is the mountain, and the goat standing at the summit with the astrological sign of Capricorn. All difficulties can be overcome and the summit reached by

66 Community 1926, Agni Yoga Society.

the divine goat - a symbol of group effort in scaling steep and arduous terrain.

It is a subsidiary Law of the Law of Magnetic Impulse and is associated with the energy of love. Disciplined progressive effort through love and selflessness—the basic principles of universal brotherhood. The consciousness of the group members begin to have a taste of universal brotherhood based on the principles of love, self-discipline and selflessness, through planned service.

The groups of servers are not formed for the purpose of perfecting the individual member in any group. This is a basic and essential statement. In these groups, the members complement and strengthen each other, and, in the aggregate of their qualities and abilities, they eventually form a bridge of light through which the spiritual energy of the soul and the Hierarchy can flow, unimpeded for the benefit of humanity.

Hitherto the spheres of daily service of individuals within groups remain as their individual dharma. But, now is being added to the effort of a group activity, a common and united service or group dharma. "Each person in such groups has to learn to work in a close mental and spiritual cooperation with all the others, and this takes time. Each has to pour forth love on all, and this is not easy. Each has to learn to subordinate his own personality ideas and his personal growth to the group requirements, for at present some will have to hasten their progress in certain directions, and some must slow it down as a service to the others. This process will take place automatically as the group identity and integration becomes the dominant thought in the group consciousness."[67] A balance

between individual and group dharma occurs as the individuals and the group finds their rhythm.

Decentralization, where nothing is asked for the separate self is key to group progress. Understanding this Law of soul life brings clarity to the relationship between a soul's purpose and group work. Decentralization will be a cornerstone of the Aquarian civilization. What is decentralization? It occurs naturally when the soul becomes the dominant factor in the life of the individual. It is decentralization of the personality in the realization of the greater Life in which all living beings are a part. It is the awakening of the soul that brings this realization.

Decentralization of a soul-infused integrated personality is one of the essential qualifications for admission into a Master's Ashram. Some of the others are: self-discipline, silence and occult serenity. Decentralization is another term for co-measurement or a sense of right proportion in which there is a just perception of one's place in the planetary chain of hierarchy.

It is through the working of this law that the group members penetrate into the meaning of the symbol for this law. The mountain's summit is not reached alone, but with one's group brothers and sisters.

The Teachers have said group progress is the result of self-imposed discipline, love and self-forgetfulness. The top of the mountain is a metaphor for self-realization. The goat is a symbol of group progress and the sign of Capricorn—a symbol for the supreme loving will, propelling all onward: "The whole life and expression of the Solar Logos will only be possible, and His purpose only be

---

[67] Alice A. Bailey, Esoteric Psychology II

revealed, when He has brought each atomic unit to the stage of self-realization."[68]

"The climb to the summit of our Kingdom is a perilous journey. Most take the endless winding road to reach the apex. Only the brave and the willful become our avid rock-climbers. For discipline, love and steadfastness outweighs the fear."[69]

39. *LAW OF EXPANSIVE RESPONSE*

This is the sixth of the seven Laws of Soul Life and the first to have a verse associated with it. This law deals with the gradual evolutionary expansion of the consciousness that dwells in every form, and therefore deals with response to environment and opportunity. This law deals with the relation ship between matter and light.

Its symbol is the flaming rosy sun with a sign in the center, a sign symbolizing the union of fire and water. Below this sign is found a hieroglyphic that indicates the Earth sign and the keynote of the planet or physical body of the Planetary Logos.

One interpretation of the symbol is that the hieroglyph resembling the Earth sign symbolizes matter. The fiery rosey hued sun which contains the two triangles for the union of fire and water symbolizes light, more specifically the blended soul-personality. Imagine a person radiating with intelligent love as the emotional and mental bodies come under the control of the soul. This law along with the seventh waits until until the first five have begun to do their work.

The energy of this law is the adaptive and expansive quality of intelligent activity guided by love. Through this law, matter and light come into relationship. This law and the seventh Law of soul life have to do with the life of the group becoming a useful unit of Hierarchical service, requiring attention and orientation to to telepathic impressions from a Master's ashram.

The Teacher DK in the book Esoteric Psychology II, places emphasis on laws six and seven of the soul laws as working closely together. "We can now, with brevity speak of them (the sixth and seventh laws) together. The other five laws have worked out into a definite activity upon the physical plane...the working out of the purpose of the Most High, upon the plane of phenomena. Dimly can the effect of the sixth and the seventh laws begin to be recognized."

These sixth and seventh laws of soul life are expressions of the purpose and life of our planetary Logos and therefore to express these two laws of soul life is to touch the underlying purpose of the "One In Whom, we live and move and have our being."

The stanza for the sixth Law of Soul Life is: "The Sun, in all its glory, has arisen and cast its beams athwart the Eastern sky. The union of the pairs of opposites produce, in the cycles of the time and space, both clouds and mists. These veil a mighty conflagration....The flood pours forth. The ark floats free...the flames devour. The three stand free; and then again the mists envelop. Above the clouds of earth, a sign shines forth....Only the eye of vision sees this sign.

---

[68] Alice A. Bailey, A Treatise on Cosmic Fire.

[69] 1994 - 1997, Letters

Only the heart at peace can hear the thunder of the Voice which issues from the dark depths of the cloud. Only an understanding of the law which elevates and lifts can teach the man of fire and son of water to enter into mist. From thence he climbs on to the mountain top and there again stands free. The triple freedom thus achieved has naught to do with earth, or water, or with fire. It is a freedom, triple in its kind, which greets the man who passes freely from the sphere of earth into the ocean of the watery sphere, and thence on to the burning ground of sacrifice. The sun augments the fire; it dissipates the mist and dries the earth. And thus the work is done."[70]

The stanza, full of symbolism, is also showing that the secret of progress to the many states of consciousness lis in sensitive awareness. As the law expansive response proceeds in the group's particular field of planned service, a parallel activity is occurring—the "burning ground," a process of intensified purification which removes personal impediments to the flow of light. Groups and their personnel advance most quickly, who meet the need of humanity and face this law squarely, with resourcefulness, flexibility and sensitive awareness.

"Do not slumber in my Kingdom or I shall awake thee with a jolt. There is no time for rest, nor relaxation. My gates only beckon the willful and courageous."[71]

40. *LAW OF THE LOWER FOUR OR ETHERIC UNION*

This seventh of the seven laws of soul life, like the sixth has a verse. It is a law relating mind to higher knowledge, meditation, the right use of the mind and mastery of the soul over four types powers: ignorance, passion, death and darkness. Its symbol is a male and female figure, standing back to back. The male form holds above his head a shield of silver, a great reflector, while the female form holds above her an urn full of oil. Below this symbol is a hieroglyphic which contains the secret of the "astral plane"[72] which must be dominated by mind.

The male and female figures symbolize the fact that nature achieves productivity through polarity. The male figure represents the mind. Through the proper use of the mind, the energies of the emotions and desires are brought under control. One interpretation of this multifaceted symbol is that the astral or emotional body once stabilized, becomes a reflector of light. Right use of mind makes the intellect a reflector of the intuition. The female figure represents Sophia or Wisdom and Higher Knowledge, ready to pour the oil, a symbol of anointing and the flow of intuition to a ready mind. The mind experiences the world as dual, as you and I, but it is also capable of sensing and revealing unity. The un-illumined mind analyzes, but the illumined mind functions intuitively and synthetically. The four powers controlling the personality once transformed and overcome results in mastery of the soul

---

[70] Alice A.Bailey, Esoteric Psychology II,

[71] 1994 - 1997, Letters

[72] A subtler realms of energy jut above the physical realm and below the mental realm. It is characterized by its fluidity.

over form and an etheric union of the soul and personality.

Meditation and right use of mind are keys to mastery. As explained by the Teacher DK through the books of Alice A. Bailey, meditation enables the brain and mind to vibrate in unison with the soul. The right use of mind is fully attentive to everything as it is, so as to fully understand our experience. It is at the heart of the Buddha's teaching.

The stanza for this law is simple but not an easy one to understand: "Four sons of God went forth. But only one returned. Four Saviors merged themselves in two, and then the two became the One."

Applying the key of geometry, four symbolizes the square or matter. The circle, the square's opposite, represents perfect unity, unmanifest spirit. Geometry is only one key of many to interpreting a written or pictorial symbol when number is involved.

The following is just one interpretation: In geometry, there is a construction problem called the "squaring of the circle". Using only a compass and straight edge, construct a square and circle, of nearly equal size resulting in a unity between the two opposite shapes. The geometric "squaring of the circle" problem and its solution "the circle squared" is a metaphor for the mystery of evolution—spirit expressing its unmanifest dimension or qualities through form.

Using the Law of Analogy to take this metaphor a step further, the squaring of the circle represents the spiritual regeneration accomplished within the human body through the union of opposites. "The circle squared" is also a symbol for the opening of the crown chakra. When the personality achieves union with the soul, spirit can then come into full expression—enlightenment.

In the above stanza it says the "four becomes the two". One interpretation of this is that the son of man overcoming the four powers is transfigured into the second person of the Trinity, a living Son of God.

The symbols and verses may only be sounding words and meaningless phrases to the average reader and student, but they have been given by the wise Teacher DK, because they contain a potency that will stimulate the higher centers. That the stanza of this law also says "the two became the one", could be pointing to that evolutionary achievement destined for humanity—the ultimate union of the fourth kingdom in nature, humanity, and the fifth or spiritual kingdom of souls.

IV

EIGHT QUALITIES OF GROUP ACTIVITY

"As birds fly together to summer realms, so souls unite in flight. Passing through the gate they thus alight before the throne of God."
-Discipleship in the New Age, Alice A. Bailey

The Eight Qualities of Group Activity developed out of inner guidance and an outer or physical journey. Three spiritual seekers, were asked by an Elder who dwells in the spiritual realm or Fifth Kingdom, if they would like to go on a 108-day journey to India, Nepal, Tibet and possibly Kashmir.

One of the three had been serving as a conscious channel to the Fifth Kingdom prior to meeting the other two. The other two spiritual seekers, an artist and an architect, had gone on group journeys guided by an Elder of Fifth Kingdom. The three had also worked together on the project mentioned in law #14. This resulted in the beginning of a group experiment.

The three agreed to the request. Soon, guidance came through about the journey. They knew the reasons were spiritual in nature but not exactly how. It wasn't until the journey's end that its true purpose was revealed.

Guidance came through detailing the itinerary. They would be on their own, unless guidance was necessary. With a year to prepare there was much to do. Departure would be next year, the year of the Hale Bopp comet, as some may remember.

Guidance directed them to the Alice A. Bailey books to study the Science of the Antahkarana. In one of the messages, guidance said this about the soul and its sojourn through matter: "The plane of matter was created to allow the Soul to understand all the experiences of being in different planes of vibration, so as to build the divine qualities of compassion, wisdom and so forth. Because our Heavenly Father's creation is just and perfect and based solely on Order and Divine Law, He created the different Laws. Simply stated, the Father wants and desires deeply to have all His creation return to the bosom of His heart. In order to see how His Divine Laws are operable, He thrusted out into His universe of creation all of Us who are sparks of Himself. This created the Law of Magnetism. If you were to think for a moment of a boomerang, you would understand this concept. The only way the Soul can return to its Source is through the personality experience, the only way the Soul can gain the overall experience of life in totality. This is the reason the plane of matter exists. It is a blessing in disguise. This is how the Soul works with the personality, only the Soul knows of your higher qualities of being a spiritual being and yes, often does not want to deal with such a primitive state."

Guidance described that the 'pilgrimage' would be divided into eight segments related to the Buddha's gift of the noble eightfold path, its symbol being a wheel with eight spokes, one for each gift. The journey came with an assignment - a question: "How does each segment hold a piece to the bigger picture of the journey?" The following guidance was given:

"The teachings of the pilgrimage shall be divided into eight segments, one for each spoke of the Wheel of Life. The disciple need not know from whence it began or finished, but should stay finely attuned to the present. Truly there is no start, nor finish as surely as there is no part of the future as measured in God Time.

Although appearing stationary, the Wheel is continually in motion."

On February 16, 1997, the three flew from the U.S. to India. The journey took them along the Ganges, to Haridwar, Gangotri, the Kulu Valley, Lucknow, Delhi, Agra, Amritsar, Ladakh, Varanasi, Bodh Gaya, Sarnath, Allahabad, Patna, Siliguri, Darjeeling, Sikkim, Kathmandu, Lhasa, Shigatse, back to Nepal and India and then home to the U.S.A. It was a beautiful experience but physically and psychologically taxing. Each segment tested the personalities to the core and their friendship had suffered.

After the full moon of in May, while in Shigatse, guidance came through that revealed the deeper purpose of the trip. Guidance informed the three that as a service group, they were useless to the Hierarchy. The three had done poorly in developing certain group qualities. Needless to say, the small group experiment had to be dissolved, for the time being.

Guidance suggested they continue their spiritual studies and this is how they became Arcane School students. Three years later they healed their friendship, to the great joy of the Elder who had proposed the trip. Looking back, the three agreed it was a rewarding experience of spiritual growth.

With the friendship "raised from the dead", they knew it was time to finish what they had started: the assignment. How did each of the eight segments hold a piece of the bigger picture of the journey? Processing and integrating the experience of the journey was transformative and productive.

It made them more aware of the importance of sacrifice, the need for purification, the need to staying connected to the octave of love—the soul, and above all, applying the Buddha's teachings on the eightfold path.

This chapter is the product of that experience, which was a life changer. As the spiritual adage goes: "The gifts of failure guarantee success when rightly understood."

The study and application of the noble eightfold path will help in adjusting the attitude of the personality to the soul and of the individual to the group and the divine laws. The *Eight Gifts* and *Eight Qualities* will serve to guide a group's unfolding soul life and support the externalization of the Hierarchy, which begins with the externalizing of the soul within.

Guidance provided five questions to help the three with processing and integrating the "trip of a lifetime":

1. "How would you expound the eight gifts of the Buddha to suit modern day humanity?"

2. "How do you see these gifts or virtues fitting into that part of the Plan We are creating for the new world?"

3. "How could you associate any of these gifts or virtues with service, and if so, in what way?"

4. "What universal law and quality of group activity would you associate with each of these gifts or virtues?"

5. "How could you further develop and expand these gifts or virtues among yourselves?"

The value of guidance from the higher realms is undeniable. But, more so, when spiritual teachings are applied and there is an ardent desire to be useful to members of the Hierarchy in the working out of the Plan.

In the contributions of individual members of a group, free will is always honored and all are equally valued. What contributes to the flowering of the group life and its planned service is what matters. It takes self-discipline to remain vigilant and decentralized. Love and Truth must always guide the group's unfolding. The eight gifts and qualities can be used as a standard of measure.

Even if a task is imperfectly or inadequately performed, when it is motivated by right aspiration, the fruit of group work has merit. Perfection isn't the goal. Aspiration towards it, is what matters.

The fruits of group activity will be the result of the soul qualities the group can achieve. The soul qualities depend upon the an application of the eight gifts and an understanding of the Divine Laws. The eight gifts, eight qualities and higher laws, are a trinity of lights that will support and nurture, group experiment, experience and expression.

Followed by the *Eight Qualities*, the *Eight Gifts* are presented first:

The Eight Gifts *(or virtues of the Buddha)*

First Gift	**Right Belief**
Second Gift	**Right Aspiration**
Third Gift	**Right Speech**
Fourth Gift	**Right Conduct or Action**
Fifth Gift	**Right Living**
Sixth Gift	**Right Effort**
Seventh Gift	**Right Mindfulness or Remembrance**
Eighth Gift	**Right Meditation or Concentration**

1. Right Belief: The truth is known because of the relationship of our little self to the greater life of the universe. The disciple is patient with sorrow and the problems of life through discrimination and right perception. Viewpoint is healthy. Understanding is healthy. Listening is healthy. Disappointment is used to rise to greater achievement. The maya of identification with matter, the astral glamours of the unreal and mental illusions, such as separation, is recognized and one is not so critical or unkind to others caught in such belief. Discernment is key here to see what is true from false so as to overcome attachments and habits. There is knowing and trust in the ultimate triumph of good and alignment with the forces of light. There is poise and steadfastness. The Law of Love strengthens Right Belief. Right belief supports the efforts of Group Polarization.

2. Right Aspiration: This is one of the more important gifts to be embodied. For a group to progress they have to be able to hold steady in the light of the soul and know that in wisdom lies choice, motive and knowing when to let go of that which has outlived its usefulness. What was true in the past changes due to greater awareness and expansion of consciousness. To study, reflect upon and apply the divine laws, one learns that with expanded and more inclusive consciousness, debated points will be clarified and assume their place. To criticize in thought or word is to lose sight of the group organism seeking to achieve useful group activity. Contradictions disappear in the light of unfolding truth as a result of the aspiration to become like our Elders in wisdom, love and compassion. It is learning to work in harmony within one's environment, not in spite of it. The aspiration to be like Christ is not a glamour. It is being honest with one's self in realizing that there is a reservoir of strength one can tap into when fortitude is lacking. This is how Christ and Buddha lived out their final years, utilizing every moment to execute the will of the divine—through every action and interaction, through every encounter and circumstance. They did not know precisely how their end would come, but were determined to fulfill the purpose of their dharma. This gift demonstrates that if activity is based on loving understanding, all are blessed by it, regardless of outcome. It is learning to be responsible for the flow of energy between oneself, the group and one's environment in harmonious, clear and coordinated ways. Pondering the Laws of Antithesis, Service and Loving Understanding will motivate Right Aspiration. Right Aspiration promotes sensitivity to truth and divine purpose thus strengthening Group Response and Discipline.

3. Right Speech: This gift teaches to speak with words of encouragement, kindness and helpfulness. Correct speech requires no waste of words. The injunction is to: "Let the words be few and kind; let them be well-chosen, and loudly spoken. Let the words be to the glory of the Great One." It is important for group activity to produce something of a creative expression and at the same time to create it through harmlessness. The etheric throat center is the creative chakra. Creativity is also the third aspect of the Soul's nature, the other two being Will and Love. In the words of one of the spiritual Elders: "Here is where the disciple learns how to imitate God as the Creator, as the quality of creativity is expressed fully in one's life. As this is completed, it fulfills the learning of the third aspect of the soul — Creativity." The Good, True and Beautiful requires creativity and harmlessness to make equivalent forms visible and vital to others. Speech is a major tool of creativity and supports positive, forward moving group activity. The Law of Group Progress will strengthen Right Speech. Right Speech supports the the group in achieving Group Integrity and Cohesion.

4. Right Conduct or Action: This gift expresses the simplicity of manner with the grace and dignity of the soul. It is to be aware of glamours such as that of mental pride and self-satisfaction which negates right action and the flow of love. It is right action which springs from love and clear thinking when faced with choice. A quiet, simple manner is exhibited, peaceful, non-combative, silent among the talkative and poised among the excited. Difficulties arise from failure to recognize the fundamental Law of Love and it subsidiary law, the Law of Karma. It is a thankful attitude for what one has received and the opportunity to give. One cannot receive without trust or faith and one cannot give without love. In the later stages of consciousness expansion, faith and trust are replaced with direct experience. It is a loving and caring attitude towards each one in the group. When one individual in the group advances, the entire group benefits. It is a dominant expression of the Kingdom of Souls and enlightened Beings who have achieved mastery over the human condition and have assumed responsibility for the evolution of planetary life. This gift has particular application to the quality of Group Radiatory Love. Meditation on the Law of Expansive Response will strengthen Right Conduct. Right Conduct is key to Group Radiatory Love.

5. Right Living: The secret of Right Living is to be willing to work for the true principles in life that one is seeking to develop. It is motivated Love, by the willingness to be in right relationship to divine will, the soul, fellow human beings, the Hierarchy, the Plan and form. It is fiery love followed by action. Christ demonstrated the gift—that of attunement and striving toward oneness with Divine Life. Buddha achieved his enlightenment through this gift. It is dependent upon a mental and intuitive grasp of the divine laws and divine purpose. Divine purpose must underly the livingness of the soul. This gift is closely connected with the Will aspect of divinity. Right Living is the antidote to fear in all its forms. In the early stages, it is faith and hope grounded in truth. In the latter stages it is consciousness grounded in reality. It is the spontaneous desirelessness of the soul which asks nothing for the separated self. It is an ardent desire that works for a world of justice and peace where humanity can fulfill its divine potential of entering the Kingdom of Souls and being responsible for the further evolution of Earth. Pondering the Seven Laws of Soul Life and the Law of Unity will strengthen Right Living. Group Rhythm which creates an invocative point of tension, is a result of unified Right Living.

6. Right Effort: This gift demands dedication to walking the spiritual path of ascent or transformation and a recognition of the Hierarchy. Right effort transfigures selfless love into an agent of divine will or fiery love. The Masters say that we must go at least half way and then They will rush to greet us. A right sense of proportion is also important to Right Effort. A preoccupation with perfection leads to extremism. There is an aphorism: "'Perfect' is the enemy of good", which means insistence on perfection without consideration of what is best for the good of the whole, often prevents implementation of good improvements. Therefore, avoid holding onto extreme views. Right effort requires the group members be knowledgeable of the spiritual path that transforms and transfigures the human being, plus the courage to tread this path to its end. This keeps the lines of communication open between the human groups and guidance from higher realms. Right Effort also asks the group members to avoid extremes. Adaptability and flexibility is a key to carrying out the Divine Plan, while keeping in mind that creation is operating in divine wisdom and higher order. Divine Perfection is the impulse driving each unit of consciousness towards its unique perfection. Strive for perfection of self through service and selflessness, with compassion for yourself and others.

The Tibetan Teacher DK has some good advise when it comes to right effort. He says, and this is a paraphrase from Discipleship in the New Age Vol. I by Alice A. Bailey, that "even if one's outer life is regimented, following a regularity, even if there are no points of crisis happening, of high moments of realization, to see to it that in the inner life there is potency and dynamic impulse, even when the outer life seems molded to a pattern. The moment a man sets his hand to the plough and starts upon his ploughing, from that moment until he has completed his task, he remains internally free but outwardly bound. So it must ever be with the servers in our work." It is one's inner orientation that matters, not the outer life when it comes to one's service to humanity or the plan.

Wisdom says there is naught but perfection—Love says there is no perfection until all is perfected. This is the motivation behind the redemptive work of the Hierarchy of Light. Meditation on the Laws of Polarity and Perfection will strengthen Right Effort. Group Intensification of Love depends upon Right Effort.

7. Right Mindfulness or Remembrance: requires elimination out of the personality of all those forms which veil the Real. These forms are either self-chosen or self-created and a part of illusion. This virtue requires a discipline to strip away the illusions and glamours. Dispelling illusion leads to a true apprehension of the soul and the power to transfer that correct perception to the brain. It is remembrance of oneself as a soul or identification with the soul. The practice of kindness is essential as well as recognizing what one has in common with others, but supremely important is to see the real light in all your brothers and sisters and fellow human beings. Appreciate nature as the ideal of Beauty and the Self as Beauty of the IDEA. A blend of the two is the aesthetic viewpoint to one's creative efforts. One achieves enlightenment through constant mindfulness. Remembrance referred to here is also knowledge accumulated in the consciousness of the soul, stored through the many incarnations and accessible as a result of this virtue. The practice of this virtue eventually leads to remembrance of the Self, the I AM, the knowing of one's true identity. Knowledge reveals it, Love embodies it, Teachings express it. Trust embraces it, and patience and detachment are needed to allow the process of mindfulness to do its work. Pondering the Law of Enlightenment will strengthen Right Mindfulness. Group Relationship is nurtured by this virtue and evokes from higher planes the necessary soul stimulation and growth.

8. Right Meditation or Concentration: The equivalent on the soul level of precise thought and visualization by the mind which builds the antahkarana. Through the antahkarana the soul can communicate with the brain through the mind, as the building of the antahkarana creates a synchronization between the three. This sometimes registers as flashes of 'intuition'.[73] Building the antahkarana takes determination, but when fully built can tap into the great reservoir of energy called the "raincloud of knowable things" as Patanjali calls it, or the Buddhic or Intuitional plane, as the ageless wisdom calls it, for purposes of precipitation through groups. The antahkarana then becomes a channel for intuitive knowing to emerge in the consciousness of the meditator. The

great purpose of meditation is to bring that which is in the world of cause seeking expression into manifestation. In time the "raincloud of knowable things" will be precipitated upon the whole of earth and humanity. A spiritual Elder has a term for this: "Dreaming straight from the heart"[74]—a dynamic inner listening conducted in a state of inner poise and silence, which is evocative. Later, proceeding from the Path of Ascent, when the Way of the Higher Evolution is tread, a template of living Light called the 'Eye of Horus'[75] is placed over the third eye of the Initiate by higher Beings. All this is brought about through meditation. The entire scheme of manifestation is brought about through organized and conscious meditative methods. Meditation on this gift and the Laws of Manifestation will strengthen Group Vision. This gift strengthens the power of silence, the evocative power of the soul and "dreaming straight from the heart".

The Eight Qualities (*of group activity*)

First Quality:	**Group Polarization**
Second Quality:	**Group Relationship**
Third Quality:	**Group Intensification of Love**
Fourth Quality:	**Group Response and Discipline**
Fifth Quality:	**Group Vision and Projection**

---

[73] Vision, direct knowing of spiritual truth, guidance and insight that is permeated with oneness, love and wholeness. It has been called the "key" to the power of the gods. Intuition always is experienced as a state of oneness.

[74] A term the Master gave and requested it be pondered deeply. It is the soul working with the intuitive realm of Buddhi.

[75] Allows the initiate to communicate with Cosmic Masters and Lords of Light in the re-genesis and redemption of physical creation. The 'Eye of Horus' will the take the form of a design element in the coming Temples of Initiation for the integration of higher vibratory patterns of light during initiatory processes in the light body of initiates.

Sixth Quality:	***Group Integration and Cohesion***
Seventh Quality:	***Group Radiatory Love***
Eighth Quality:	***Group Rhythm***

1. Group Polarization: The individual members are polarizing from emotional and mental levels to that of the soul and Kingdom of Souls. Group life is polarizing and is developing in obedience to divine law through Right Belief. Deep listening, discernment of truth, higher guidance and its acceptance, that is trusting in the guidance of spiritual Elders of the Hierarchy are characteristics of group polarization. One of the qualities that the Hierarchy looks for in those who are in process of polarizing, is a willingness to cooperate with the Kingdom of Souls on new and challenging projects without astral glamor or mental illusion. The psychic life of a disciple is a definite part of his or her spiritual expression. This requires the ability to direct the mind towards elevated goals and an abiding trust in the guidance from higher realms. Meditation on the gift of Right Belief and the Law of Love will strengthen Group Polarization. Group Effect: stability, joy and peace, polarization in the soul and Kingdom of Souls, freedom from astralism, service sanely and safely performed through right orientation, safe psychic unfoldment.

2. Group Relationship: The group life is embracing and embodying a peaceful and acquiescing vibratory frequency in cooperating with one another as souls. Group members are working in harmonious relationship with one another as souls. It is a quality that comes from a willingness to submit to the rigors of the purificatory process. Out of this group quality a SERVER is born who is an inspiration to others as a result of consciousness and experience. Uppermost in the mind of the group members must be the good of the group with a proportionate attention and sensitivity to group members and their evolutionary development. In becoming the Path itself, the disciple knows what is in his fellow human being and has expanded the range of his or her endeavors. A love of truth and pure love develops within the group life. An impersonal love develops that rejoices where there is response, but looks not for it, and loves steadily, quietly, and deeply. This quality fosters the happiness of the individual and the group, a happiness closer to joy, based on confidence of the God within. Forgetfulness of self, control of the lower self and the elimination of desire of the lower self, creates the space for Joy to flow into one's being, the group life and out into the world through service. The key lies in becoming the Path itself. Meditation on Right Mindfulness, the Law of Service, and Law of Detachment will strengthen Group Relations. Group Effect: overcoming of difficulties, adherence to group good balanced by sensitivity to individual group members., group happiness, service infused with joy.

3. Group Intensification of Love: Effort is being made in the group life to rise from selfishness to selflessness as the purpose of the Kingdom of Souls to manifest soul love is realized. Greater usefulness, creativity and the power of expression is being realized through identification with the soul and Hierarchy. Group Love is that inclusive, non-critical, magnetic comprehension and attitude which in group work preserves the group integrity, fosters the group rhythm and permits no secondary personality happenings or attitudes to mar the group work. What Hierarchy is aiming for through this quality of group activity is the creation of a welcoming vibration on the part of groups whose potency will embrace incarnate human beings, and allow Christ's Ashram to channel divine love from higher realms into the world. True group love is of the highest importance. There is no difference between group love and group good. There has to be a stream of light ascending from out of the growing darkness of the material world to meet the descending stream of lighted energy from the Ashram, to enable the cooperation between human and spiritual realms. The Plan depends on there being a resonance of vibrational frequencies to allow for the descent of Hierarchy into the world. Meditation on Right Effort and the Law of Co-Creation will intensify Group Love. Group love creates the space for loving intelligent life, loving intelligent consciousness, and loving intelligent activity from Hierarchical levels to flow into every phase of group livingness, group expression and group action. Group Effect: true group love, conformity with group good, an environment in which Hierarchy can work in the world, expansion of group usefulness, group livingness, expression and action is strengthened.

4. Group Response and Discipline: This is one of the major qualities. The springing forth of a unified group commitment to the carrying out of a Hierarchical request requires mental discipline and inner listening. Aspiration to utilize ones's life for a higher purpose is becoming a living goal. No glamour is associated with this type of aspiration as it is not emotional but comes from personality-soul effort, discipline and self-control. It is an aspiration in which the personality expression bends to become Christ-like, impersonal, transformed into spiritual devotion devoid of glamor, focussed on human welfare and adherence to the Plan. The group idealism springs from non-emotional, soul sensitivity to truth and divine purpose. The quality that Hierarchy looks for is the personality's capacity to conform to the soul's aspiration to serve according to one's ability. It is a willingness of its members to tread the path of self-transformation. There is a mustering of the will to carry on fulfilling a purpose even when strengths and capacities seem frail. Groups are fields for Hierarchical expression, but groups must demonstrate in assignments, a readiness that the expenditure of force on Hierarchy's part is warranted by group effort. Group work in the new era will be the new approach to God or to Hierarchy. Meditation on the gift of Right Aspiration, the Law of Service and Law of Antithesis will strengthen Group Response. Group Effect: stabilized love, non-glamoured group idealism, strengthening of group purpose and service.

5. Group Vision and Projection: Personal vision is surrendered to the higher vision of the Plan resulting in responsive cohesion as a group. This quality will be responsible for producing the manifestation of the Kingdom of God on earth, the great necessity being vision and living organization. The vision of the Plan to be consciously sensed is the responsibility of each group member. This brings about an orientation of the group life to the life and purpose of the whole, the Kingdom of God as it exists on subtler realms in the effort to exteriorize it. The vision is held steady in the light by the group. Thought projection of the group vision proceeds unanimously from the higher mental plane to make the vision a fact upon the plane of manifestation. The new era will see visioning groups emerging. It is a great achievement of group work which requires patience. Perfection in the case of group vision is not an idealistic emotional vision, but use of the mental instrument balanced with love through identification with the soul to grasp the vision of the unfolding plan of God. This quality fosters an at-one-ment with Hierarchy and the capacity to help humanity express love. The gift of Right Meditation and pondering the Law of Co-Creation will strengthen Group Vision and Projection. Group Effect: patience, capacity to co-create with Hierarchy the new world of Aquarius.

6. Group Integrity and Cohesion: The life of the group mind should be held high on the plane of the soul with the constant building in of the third creative aspect of intelligent activity through love. This quality is again the responsibility of each group member. It is a recognition by the group member that it is a part of a Divine Life, feeling impelled to evolve and thereby expand its field of service. It is the radiatory presence of the Christ that will inspire the recognition of love unity and harmonious human relations. The group members are learning the meaning of cohesion, by recognizing the Law of Cohesion in themselves. In the new era through direct interaction with members of the spiritual Hierarchy, these recognitions will deepen into the realization that it is the love of the ALL that holds the All together. From this consciousness of inner unity, group work is transformed. When the integrity of the group is intact, the harmony of the group is

preserved and the group moves forward. Forward movement generates courage and is the antidote to discouragement. Group members use the gift of right speech in their lives and group life while treading the path of transformation. This combination generates wisdom and the members learn to apply wisdom with right speech - a great achievement along the path of transformation. Meditation on the gift of Right Speech, the Law of Cohesion and Law of Sacrifice will strengthen Group Integrity. Group Effect: forward movement, the recognition of synthesis, the right use of speech in the manifestation of truth.

7. Group Radiatory Love: It is not happy relations between group individuals but a mature group love based on a blending of soul identification and the spiritual will to serve the Plan. It is living and cooperating as souls where all are appreciated and all are equally important. This quality begins with soul identification, the stage of awareness that endows the individual with the capacity to see in their fellow co-workers, their "nature" as souls. It includes the motivation to help, non-judgmentally, those who are passing through the burning ground, that purificatory phase of group work, in whatever ways possible. It is opening to the radiatory influence of the Christ and realm of souls. The laws of life provides the opportunity of growth for all. Every form is a symbol which encases divinity seeking growth to some degree. It is group recognition of the fact that Spirit is within all form and has endowed all with the same promise of growth into Identity. All that a group uses in its activity comes to be appreciated. Everything has consciousness to some degree. This is a quality that imbues group work with spiritual Beauty which is an expression of Unity. Beauty has the power to eradicate sorrow, dispel ignorance and awaken compassion through its unity and harmony. The cosmic Ray of Harmony, in 2025, is due to come into activity and will affect humanity and the planet. It will aid in resolving conflict because it is the nature of this energy to bring harmony out of chaos, where ever unresolved chaos exists in the consciousness of humanity. During the Aquarian Age, a higher level of Beauty will manifest—the beauty of Unity and Truth, as more of humanity learns how to transmute chaos into harmony, to live as souls within form and transform conflict (opposition) into complements (cooperation). Harmony also pertains to the middle way, which leads to the realization of synthesis through a true understanding of the seeming nature of duality. It also applies to wonderful new possibilities for humanity in building the new world of Aquarius. When the group experiences the radiatory glow of love, it also experiences the radiatory influence of the Christ and Planetary Logos. This energizes and strengthens the magnetic link between group members and groups around the world, which in turn creates a unifying effect between humanity and the spiritual Hierarchy, which in turn sensitizes humanity to higher radiatory influences. Meditation on Right Living, Right Conduct and Right meditation and the Law of Perfection will strengthen Group Radiatory Love. Group Effect: compassion, appreciation of true beauty, coherency as an expression of will and purpose motivated by love, right living, high thinking and loving activity.

8. Group Rhythm: The group life through adherence to a three stage rhythmic cycle, explained later, is attaining a potency through forward moving and ashramic recognition, producing a 'point of tension'. The group fusion and rhythm causes a focussing of all the group's aims and desires dynamically upon the mental plane where a "point of tension"[76] manifests, created when the invocative power of this focalized point becomes capable of evoking response from soul and buddhic levels, of that which is seeking manifestation. The group is beginning to function as a creative Hierarchical unit. It indicates the group is approaching initiation. The point of tension is not the goal. The goal is revelation of that which is seeking to manifest from the "raincloud of knowable things". All creative processes proceed with cyclic rhythm. The creative process of groups that conform to the rhythmic cycle of creation is governed by the number three. In the first stage, the group lays emphasis upon the activity of the manifesting principle, consolidating that with which they have to work. In the second stage, the clarity and the quality of the group note to be sounded by that which is seeking manifestation, must appear and be heard. In the third stage, behind the form, that which is expressing itself through the quality and livingness and the group life emerges for all to see. If groups follow this rhythm of creation, much strain and failure will be avoided. Group rhythm is like a three stage rocket. Each stage is preparatory for the next stage, and the final stage carrying the payload or capsule, the goal of the rocket. Groups must bear this in mind. The keynote of the

---

[76] This is not a tension due to lack or mental pressure, but the group's meditative life able to hold a state of inner silence and poise, identified on soul levels with the Plan and Kingdom of Souls.

first stage is consolidation. That of the second stage must be clarity whilst the keynote of the third stage must be the making of a definite impact upon the consciousness of humanity, by the sounding and the emphasizing of some one clear note. What is yet to be revealed is how time-based rhythm will translate when Earth moves out of the physical plane and onto the etheric plane. Rhythm will still govern in the new era, only it will not be experienced as a linear time-based event. Meditation on Right Living, the Laws of Manifestation and the Law of Rhythm will strengthen Group Rhythm. Group Effect: group rhythm lading to a point of tension, unified rhythm, strengthening of the creative process through cyclic rhythm, revelation seeking precipitation.

"It is only when spiritual concepts become realities in consciousness that they really serve their purpose." -The Noble Eight-Fold Path, Manly Palmer Hall.

~

"Groups are forged in the fires of divine love" -K Messages, https://www.callfromthemountain.net

V
A BANNER FOR THE NEW ERA

We shall carry the banners of the New Age within our hearts and build with Beauty, Love and Truth.

*S*ince time immemorial, there have been banners bearing a symbol. Banners and flags have been found to date as far back as pre-dynastic Egypt and China. In the last century between World Wars I and II, a banner was created to spread the message of peace and brotherhood through the protection of humanity's cultural achievements. Called the Banner of Peace, it gained international recognition and will be explained in more detail later.

In astronomy, there is what is call the precession of the equinoxes, or the entry of the sun into each of the twelve constellations, approximately every 2,000 years, when the sun's ecliptic crosses the earth's celestial equator, in March at the time of the equinox. It takes 25,000 years or a Great Solar Age for our sun to precess or go through all twelve constellations.

From the perspective of the higher realms, each time the sun enters another constellation, it brings with it a cosmic influence lasting approximately 2,000years. Thus, every 2,000 year cycle carries with it the influence of that particular constellation. The 2,000 year Piscean cycle now ending as Earth enters Aquarius.

However, celestial mechanics is no guarantee that humanity will evolve in terms of spiritual potential, due to free will and choice. Which is why humanity's evolutionary progress has not been along more spiritual lines.

Nevertheless, the cosmic gears continue to turn. Not only is one solar age ending and another beginning, but our entire solar system is spiraling onto a higher level of expression. What this means is, Earth is in a state of unprecedented flux. The Piscean age has produced the climaxing civilization characterized by personality aims and goals. Aquarius, the age that earth is now moving into will be characterized by justice, unity and love. Synchronous with this 2,000 year Aquarian cycle, our solar system has just entered a galactic Aquarian Cycle of 25,000 years. The synchronization of earth's 2,000 year Aquarian cycle with the galactic 25,000 year Aquarian cycle is magnifying the unprecedented spiritual awakening within portions of humanity.

The Banner of Peace (Fig. 1) with its message of peace was a forcrunner, nearly 100 years ago of this spiritual awakening to Aquarian values. The banner was conceived in 1929 by the Russian artist, writer and philosopher Nicholas Roerich, who, after witnessing the senseless destruction in World

Banner of Peace (FIG. 1)

War I, of great libraries, cathedrals and art treasures, wanted to preserve humanity's cultural achievements and prevent a repeat. Institutions, museums, etc. would identify themselves by flying the banner for this purpose.

The Banner of Peace uses the universal language of geometry in its symbolism of of brotherhood, peace and unity. On a white background is a circle representing unity. Inside the circle are three "amaranth"[77] spheres in the form of a triangle representing the trinity of Deity found in all major

---

[77]The reddish amaranth is considered in various folk cultures and traditions a symbol of Brotherhood.

religions. This banner was placed over cultural monuments and its message of peace planted seeds that sprouted in the hearts and minds of many. It attracted the attention of influential intellects and helped awakened the idea of brotherhood among peoples.

The Banner of Peace earned Roerich a nomination for the Nobel Peace Prize, the first time an artist has ever been honored. Nicholas and his wife Helena traveled extensively promoting the principles of brotherhood and goodwill. They were over-lighted by an Elder of the spiritual Hierarchy - the Master Morya.

In 1995, 66 years after Nicholas Roerich conceived the Banner of Peace, another Elder of the Spiritual Hierarchy, the Master K.H., transmitted the following verse:

"Three circles within a circle Thou hast been given to cherish. It depicts new thought for the coming New Age. Hark! There shall be a new symbol given which will signify a new consciousness, a new school of thought, a banner of peace, and establish Christ upon earth, within and without. Verily, I say it is upon you soon."

The Masters Morya and K.H. work closely together and are known for their love, wisdom, compassion and service to humanity. They have a fondness for poetic verse. It is a wonderful way to dispense teachings, words of wisdom and guidance. It serves to keep the spiritual seeker ardently searching for the truth.

The first two sentences of the above verse is referring to the Roerich Banner of Peace and the seeds it has planted in consciousness. The remaining two sentences are referring to an imminent new symbol,

which the three co-authors call: "A Banner for the New Era", for the new seeds of light it will plant in the consciousness of an awakening humanity.

Overall Symbolism of "A Banner for the New Era" (p. 106): The outer tricolored circle represented by the violet is the marriage of spirit and matter, the gold represents the Christ Consciousness and the indigo blue represents the energy of Love-Wisdom which governs our Solar System. The circle of three colors symbolizes the eternal oneness. The three images inside the circle which were the "amaranths," of the Banner of Peace symbolize in "Banner for the New Era", the three planetary centers: Shamballa, Hierarchy and Humanity whose interplay will come into greater manifestation during the new age. The four golden spheres outside the tricolored circle represent the four quadrants of the universe and their relationship The background of violet indicates the seventh ray, the dominant ray of the Aquarian cycle, whose influence will always be in the background. The terms "new consciousness, "new school of thought" and "Christ upon earth, within and without..upon you soon" are in reference to the earth's unprecedented physical transition into a higher realm of spiritual existence.

Symbolism of Humanity (fig. 2): the design is attributed to Foster Bailey, a disciple of the Teacher DK and their collaboration. The indigo-blue circle represents the life of our Solar Logos. There are three cosmic Beings symbolized by the triangle, one of

Humanity:
the manifest realm of Earth where the Plan is worked out through intelligent love. **(fig. 2)**

whom is the Buddha, Who stand behind the coming World Teacher, symbolized by the five pointed star. They are aiding the Christ's work to humanity. The equal armed cross, of cosmic origin, has informed all the cross symbology as perceived and used by humanity down through the ages. The function of this symbol or figure is to carry the frequency of the soul of humanity and Kingdom of Souls into outer expression. Guidance instructed the symbol or figure of Humanity should take the place of one of the "amaranths".

Symbolism of Hierarchy (fig. 3): This figure is called the *Universalis Infinitum*, from the Latin universalis "of or belonging to all," and the Latin infinitum "endlessly". It replaces one of the other "amaranths" in the Banner of Peace. It represents the "new consciousness" for humanity and "Christ upon earth within and without". The rose and deep blue represent the Love and the Will, respectively of Christ, the World Teacher. The green represents our Mother, the earth and the responsibility of humanity for Her well-being. The geometry of the Universalis Infinitum is to be a template for a university of Light in the new era. At the points of the twelve-pointed star will be new schools of thought. The golden-yellow inner

Hierarchy:

the spiritual realm of perfected souls where the Love of God is known, in process of externalizing and who are the custodians of the Plan. **(fig. 3)**

circle and its central dot symbolizes the God-

Force of our Planetary Logos and His expression in Shamballa, Sanat Kumara, the Lord of the World. The center is reserved for ceremonial functions.

Symbolism of Shamballa (fig. 4): Taking the place of the third amaranth in the Banner of Peace, this symbol or figure represents Shamballa with its Council Chamber comprised of the Christ, highly evolved members of the spiritual Hierarchy, Devic Kingdom, and extraplanetary cosmic Light-Beings, aiding the work of the Christ and Planetary Logos. It holds the diamond perfection of Logoic Will and Purpose. It is the only one of the three figures with four points extending beyond its circumference, veiling a mystery. One of points touches the

Shamballa:

the highest spiritual realm of Earth where the Will of God is known and utilized to fulfill the purpose of planetary evolution. **(fig. 4)**

center of the tricolored outer circle. The 4 outer points plus the 8 spheres total 12. The length of the four inner points to the four outer points is derived from one of the proportioning cornerstones of ancient geometry called the "sacred cut"[78]. Eight is the higher octave of four. When these three numbers four, eight and twelve are added together, they total the number twenty four, the number of Shamballa. Four is the octave of manifestation, eight is the octave of the Christ and twenty four is the octave of Shamballa. Figure 4 is therefore a synthesis of all three octaves.

---

[78] the "sacred cut" is based on the number seven and is found in the architecture of the pyramids and ancient temples.

To conclude this chapter, the Aquarian Age will be an age in which group consciousness flowers and when many wonders of the new earth will be manifested.

There will be many symbols and banners of wisdom in the new age. It must be remembered that spiritually designed symbols transcend their literal interpretation.

It is the expansion of consciousness, the unifying power of love, vision, cooperation, and the divine Law of our own being that will characterize the new age of Light and its wondrous expressions. As the following words state:

"The banners of the new brotherhood are flying upon the Earth. Mankind has his homeland in sight and shall be brought there. You shall go out and cover the earth because that is where your consciousness shall be as it continually expands until you are the Earth in your love, in your vision and in the breadth and depth and heights of your being. Go in oneness. Go in Peace."[79]

EPILOGUE

Is it necessary to know about the divine laws, the eight gifts (of the Buddha), the eight qualities of group activity, or a banner for the new era? Is self-transformation at this time of spiritual awakening necessary? The Epilogue will attempt to answer these questions.

The problems of humanity and the turbulent conditions the planet is experiencing are but the outer or superficial expressions of a deeper underlying cause: the human mind—a mind that is destroying the world due to disregard for divine law and divinity itself. Just as ignorant or un-illumined minds can destroy, illumined minds can heal, restore and create in life supporting ways. This is the dichotomy of human potential.

The voice of the soul has been stirring within the human heart for a long time, crying there is an emptiness, a void that needs to be filled. The three recognitions: 1. The reality of the soul, 2. The existence of loving, wise and compassionate beings in a higher realm and, 3. The divine plan with its nurturing divine laws, are entering human consciousness and filling the void with renewed hope in the future, and faith in the human capacity to evolve.

It will eventually be realized that the problems of the world are the responsibility of all humanity, that we are responsible for the consequences of our actions, that divine laws exist and that consciousness precedes form.

Humanity can choose the upward arc of evolution or remain stuck in the old patterns of the past. In choosing the former, humanity will awaken to the great Law of Cause and Effect, and will begin to share in the common spiritual view of responsibility.

This realization will be a game changer for humanity. The Elders of the Fifth Kingdom have said that when this soul awakening reaches a critical mass (and it will), humanity will have stepped onto the path of transformation and will transform the life of the world, not by blindly accepting authority, but by the transformation of consciousness. Self-transformation comes from contact with the soul, the true self that lives within us all.

---

[79] Laws of Manifestation, David Spangler (message from the Lord of Civilization)

Jesus' words: "Follow me" was a message of empowerment towards self-transformation. He did not mean for anyone to follow him blindly. What he meant was to follow the divine pattern of self-transformation, he himself followed. To follow Jesus or any of the enlightened Ones is to tread the path they tread, that leads to the son of man becoming a Son of God. This has been the eternal message of the Ageless Wisdom.

Gandhi knew this when he said the way to change the world is through self-transformation. The first step is the hardest, but thats how it works, one step at a time. No teacher, politician, scholar, theologian, businessmen or scientist can do it for us.

All forms are forms of energy, whether animate or inanimate and they are interconnected through an intricate web of life. Forms of energy includes one's thoughts, words and actions. Humanity benefits or is harmed by the actions of each person, which is why each person's thoughts, words, actions and deeds matter.

This is a universal moral and ethical principle that flows from the divine Law of Love and its complementary law, the Law of Cause and Effect. In Alice A. Bailey's Discipleship in the New Age (Vol. I) it says that "The will-to-love means the love of the greater Whole and the ability to do that which is needed for the common good in the right way and with the needed skill in action".

As stated in the Introduction: "The Laws express the Will of God and lead to the manifestation of divine purpose throughout His many universes. These Laws, supporting constancy since the beginning of all creation, ordain and nurture the divine plan and responsibly work in cooperation with one another to sustain harmony among all universal existences. This is called Divine Wisdom operated by Divine Love. All creation is governed by Law."

The Divine Laws remain and operate and cannot be abandoned or neglected, they are a part of being, no matter what level of being one is on. Being expresses itself on all levels of manifestation and Divine Law expresses itself on all levels of being.

Every person has within, the ability to be an agent of love and light, contributing to the evolution of all life on this planet, in ways similar to how the Elders of the Fifth Kingdom contribute to humanity's spiritual evolution. By consciously working together, humanity can actively participate with the Fifth Kingdom in the creation of a new world.

If you are attracted to the spiritual path, or are already on it, or want to know more about it as it relates to the new era, if you are attracted to the values embodied by the enlightened ones or the ageless wisdom, or want to expand your understanding of spiritual reality, or if you are concerned about living in this time of transition, causing you to search for answers or reason, or if you simply desire a just and better world, then you may agree, that the answer to the above questions is, yes!

The message of this book is that the power of illumined minds, motivated by love, truth and shared responsibility is what will transform the world, and prepare humanity for the new era.

Suggestions for Further Reading on the Three Recognitions

atreeoflight.org A resource on the soul, the spiritual path that leads to the new era, the plan and cooperation between the Fifth Kingdom and the Fourth Kingdom of humanity, with an abundance of shareable and beautiful co-creations, writings from higher guidance, an excellent glossary of terms and more.

unveilingthespiritualpath.org A booklet from members of the Fifth Kingdom revealing the journey of self-transformation that is at the heart of all true paths and spiritual traditions. It lays the groundwork for entering the new era, while touching on the three recognitions, divine law and more.

thecomingone.org A series of articles from members of the Fifth Kingdom on what they would like awaiting humanity to know about The Coming World Teacher. "In these times of world transition, there is a need to expand our understanding of the Avatar of Love." It touches on a central aspect of the divine plan for humanity.

newwavesoflight.org This site is the result of a request from spiritual Elders to a group of human souls who responded to their call to make the three recognitions more accessible to the public. It contains beautiful co-creations that are sharable on the the Soul, the Kingdom of Souls or Fifth Kingdom, the divine plan for humanity, and more. This website was the first of its three companion websites above.

Note: In the new era, groups will receive instruction in symbol and the symbolic method for the awakening of the intuition on the functional levels of expanded consciousness. "Symbol and the Symbolic" by R.A. Schwaller de Lubicz is recommended reading on the intuitive approach to symbol. Its an eye opener and may have to be read more than once.

www.ingramcontent.com/pod-product-compliance
Lightning Source LLC
Chambersburg PA
CBHW081313150726
48001CB00022B/3041